I would like to dedicate this book to 1
me and has endured far more than she should have married to a
this workaholic! Without her support I would not have achieved
half of what I have.

Kids I love you.

A massive thanks you to my Loving Social Media team, both
past and present.

I hope you enjoy the book.

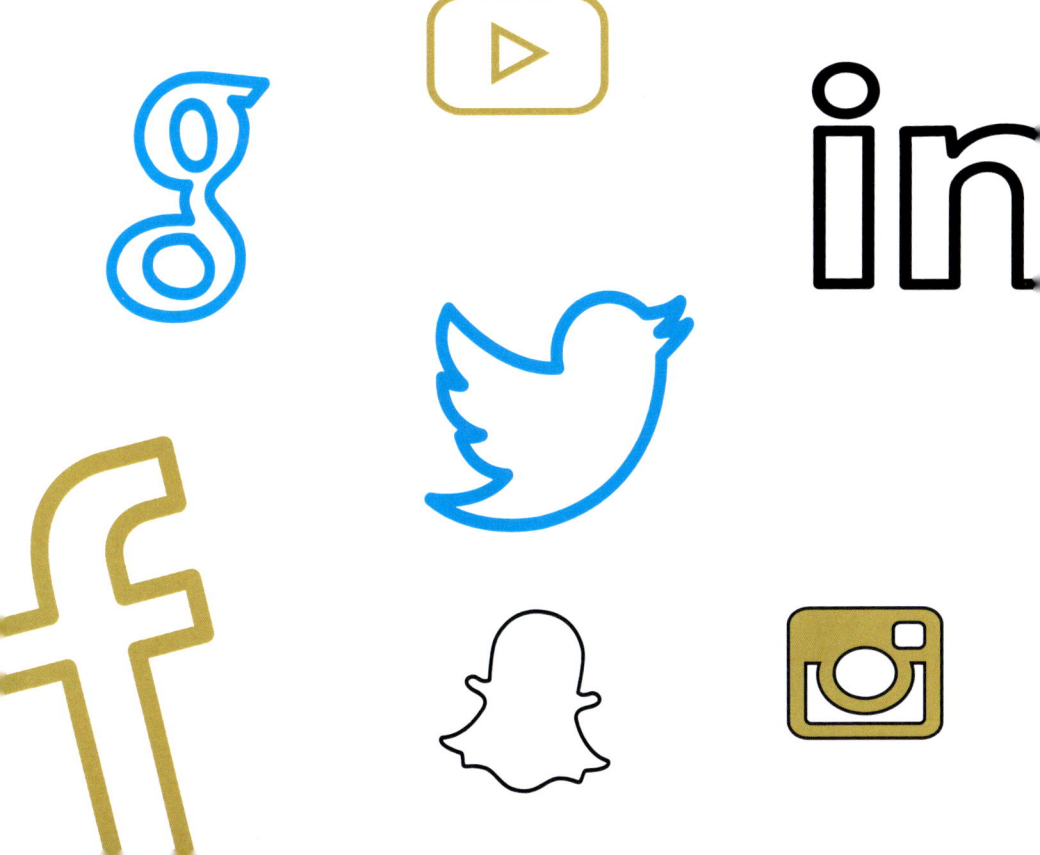

ACKNOWLEDGEMENTS

This is the second edition of a book that took four years to get to print and into your hands. Social media is certainly a passion, but writing a book has not come naturally to me!

100% Optical 2016 was the perfect place to launch my first book and following its success, it make sense that 100% Optical 2017 will be the best place to introduce 'blink' two.

I'd like to initially thank my wife, Lia. I couldn't have done this without her continued support and encouragement. She is my rock and I am truly lucky to have her.

Thank you to my Loving Social Media Team, Gemma Kennedy, Matthew Pessoa, Jordan M Tetley, Pazbi Zavatzki and Sev Safer. Their dedication is inmeasurable.

I drove my GoodLooking Optics Team crazy when I first discovered my love for social media. I could absolutely not live without their fun, energy and enthusiasm for optics.

Sinita Shah, my right hand lady, amazes me every day with her zest for life and humour and I appreciate her contribution, along with Lewis Lodge, Jake Crouch and Carmel Sanders.

Gemma Kennedy and her project management skills have been like a breath of fresh air. This company would not be where it is now without her.

Contributing to 'blink' two are my good friends Sev Safer, Graham Martin, Jordan M. Tetley, Tara Husband, and Pazbi Zavatzki,

Sev is an amazing talented blogger and I am really delighted with her contribution to this book.

Graham turned his YouTube videos into the perfect platform to raise his profile as the world's top recruiter.

Pazbi is a solid web developer, with a breadth of knowledge that is always helpful and surprising.

My stress levels have been kept down by the loving Jordan M Tetley, who has put her full heart in to editing this book. Her brilliant ideas and designing skills have created a second book I am proud of.

I thank God for Brian Tompkins, always the innovative optometrist who leads our profession.

I am also grateful to Ian Cameron for his feedback. He will always be the Clinical Optometry Heavyweight.

Three years ago I lost my dad. 2014 was not a good year for me, but, I hope that if he were still with us, he would be proud of me.

Sujan Shah kindly asked me to help with the Gary Vanerchuck project, bringing the great man to the UK.

Imran Hakim believed in me and took me to Dubai. I'm also grateful for his continual supporting and innovation in the independent sector in optics.

Thank you to Tim Nicolaou, the wee guy John Plachetka and my mum for her belief in me.

I cannot miss out Gary Vanerchuck and Tony Robbins. They have motivated and inspired me throughout.

I hope you enjoy and learn from 'blink' two.

CONTENT

- 6 INTRODUCTION
- 8 KING/QUEEN
- 10 THE MUFFIN

OPTOMETRY

- 12 DIGITAL OPTOMETRY
- 14 HEALTHY EYES

FACEBOOK

- 15
- 21 FACEBOOK LIVE

TWITTER
- 24

YOUTUBE
- 29

INSTAGRAM
- 35

MARKETING

- 38 OFFLINE MARKETING
- 40 EMAIL MARKETING
- 41 THREE TYPES OF MARKETING

BRANDING
- 44
- 46 5 TOP TIPS IN BRANDING
- 48 WHY DO YOU NEED A WEBSITE?
- 50 INNOVATION

SOCIAL STRATEGIES

- 53 SOCIAL MEDIA STRATEGY
- 54 SOCIAL MEDIA FUNNEL

55 TIME ON INVESTMENT

SOCIAL INSIGHT

56 DIGITAL TECHNOLOGY
58 SEARCH ENGINE OPTIMISATION
60 TREND JACKING
62 EXTROVERT AND INTROVERT
64 CYBERCRIME
66 SOCIAL MEDIA ^{vs} LEGAL RESPONSIBILITY

SOCIAL MEDIA

67 SNAPCHAT
68 BLOGS / THE WORLD OF BLOGGING
74 YELP
75 PINTREST

76 FAQS

81 THREE PERCEPTUAL CHANNELS
82 CHEAT SHEETS

EVALUATION

84 MEASURING YOUR SUCCESS
87 HELPFUL LINKS
89 GLOSSARY
92 HALL OF FAME
93 STRATEGY PULLOUT
97 ABOUT THE AUTHOR

INTRODUCTION

Do me a favour and do yourself a favour.
DON'T SKIP THIS SECTION!

"Social Media and Digital for Opticians" is for entrepreneurs, people with drive, ambition and obviously for the great people that work in and around optics!

As the second edition of the world's first book specialising in social media for the optical industry, I feel a sense of responsibility. Whilst wanting you to enjoy reading this book, it is imperative that you take action and execute the concepts. It's an easy read, but for the words in this book to have any value you still need to act.

If you are able to implement even a third of the advice, you will find communication improves, your customer service becomes world class and profits skyrocket. You may even avoid an unnecessary appointment with the General Optical Council! For some of you, this book may be your first foray into this new age technology. You have gone against popular belief held just a few years ago that the digital world will never affect Optics, whether positive or negative. For the uninitiated, you are in for an adventure into a whole new world.

So, who am I to feel qualified and experienced enough to offer advice?

My name is Garry Kousoulou and I have been a dispensing optician for 20+ years. I first realised the power of digital marketing when I used the platforms Myspace and Facebook to successfully get myself elected to the board of the Association of British Dispensing Opticians (ABDO). I owe a big debt of gratitude to ABDO (even though they don't realise it). It was thanks to social media that I was elected against the odds and was subsequently recognised by a Times website in 2008 as one of the top 100 people on social media.

Not realising what I had achieved, I was flattered when approached by friends to look after their social media business accounts. Over time, I employed staff and created a digital agency called Loving Social Media. It is so rewarding looking after so many opticians' digital presence, from small practices to multinational organizations. Delivering the world's first CET on social media at 100% Optical in 2014, made me the proudest optician in the world, not to mention giving talks all over the globe from Scotland to Dubai!

I have seen such a change in the way people communicate and the business market itself, over the last 20 years. I think about when I was courting my girlfriend (now my wife) in the early days; the only way of speaking to her was a landline. We both had no idea what each other was up to when we were apart, unlike now where we have social media monitoring our every move. The

invention of smartphones means we are always able to contact one another 24/7 through social media. This also means the reach of "word of mouth" is faster and 4 dimensional. Yellow pages has fallen from top spot for finding a local business to bottom. This means the way we communicate has changed and the way we build relationships has shifted online. So we really are in a situation where we need to evolve or be out of date.
I run an opticians that has heavily

> **COMPLACENCY IS NOT AN OPTION!**

invested time and resources into Digital Marketing- Search Engine Optimisation (SEO), social media and email marketing. If you are a small to medium sized business, the digital world really represents a huge opportunity where you can outmanoeuvre the bigger corporates; and I am going to show you how. You can dip in and out of this book, concentrating on one platform and discipline at a time. For complete beginners, I highly recommend starting a chapter, practicing the content, and only then moving to another chapter. Moving to the "Frequently Asked Questions" section should allay your fears and be the encouragement you need to start on your journey. There is a digital marketing plan in the middle of the book which gives you tried and tested examples, month on month, that you can easily follow.

However you got your hands on this book, you are leading the way, and at the time of this book being published you are way out in front! You will get a return on investment for your time, while keeping your reputation safe and increasing your credibility. The book is a great start. For absolute guaranteed results I totally encourage you to continue on your own with the help of the people suggested. Listen to the podcasts, browse and subscribe to the recommended websites.

This topic is one element of the future of optics and surely the preferred choice of communication with our patients, young and old, in a period of time not too far away.

> "Our only sustainable commercial advantage is to learn faster in our changing world and implement"
> Tony Robbins

This book 'blink' two has a few new pages and is 100% upto date on content. Looking at social media advancement and the changing of times.

Garry Kousoulou is hoping "Social Media and Digital for Opticians" 'blink two' is the most valuable, entertaining and eye-opening read this year.

Nearly 2.5 billion people have social media accounts!

Garry Kousoulou

CONTENT IS KING

Content creation drives digital media. Some interesting facts: a blog post has 600-800 words, Facebook's ideal post length would be about 110 words and, of course, a tweet only has 140 characters (soon to be changing to 1000). THE KING THINKS HE'S IN CHARGE OF THE CASTLE!! Content has been king and thats the way it has always been.

CONTENT

Content may be King but the
QUEEN RULES THE CASTLE

However many words are used, it doesn't come anywhere near the effectiveness of engaging with your audience. **If you want to leave your circle of influence and meet new people, retweet or like and share a post!** Engagement is the KEY! This is the new way of doing things.

MOST IMPORTANT PAGE OF THE BOOK

ENGAGEMENT

THE MUFFIN
BY J. M. ROBBINS

Everyone Has A Story In Life!

A park bench, nothing special about it. Just where I decided to sit for lunch today, surrounded by fleeting business men and women working, tourists filling up their memory cards with photos. The world never stops turning even when I take a break.

It also never stops interacting although, I thought, taking a bite out of my home-made muffins, the meaning of the word has changed. People used to talk, grab a coffee and have lunch meetings. It used to be the only way to express our points, offer business proposals, meet new people. The world was a lot smaller back then, it was harder to keep in touch with friends from the next town over, now my best-friend lives in Germany.

A woman rushes passed me, making me wonder if she might be late, if I might be late. Checking my watch, I breathe once again. You'd think with communication being easier, which in turn makes processing information faster, that work days would have been made shorter. That a day would be more relaxing, less hectic. This isn't the case: the world instead has before faster. If communication is faster, then why should filing papers be the same? If you can have a Skype call instead of a lunch meeting, then why not shorten lunch breaks?

It makes senses, although there is still something that doesn't sit right in my stomach, and it isn't my home-made muffins, no they are the best. Today I could just see a mass of different people, in a way that I hadn't been bothered to see before. It wasn't because of where they were from, or their age, or even the colour their of skin: it was how they wished to connect with the world. Interact with each other. Times have changed, but people haven't: some will still sit there reading a newspaper, others would be googling news on their phones. It's weird to sit back and see how each person is connected to the next.

"There are invisible, digital lines, connecting all of us to each other." The voice came from the right of me. I didn't notice the person sit down. Although his words were true, he snapped me out of my wondering trance.

His eyes also see the lines: so I'm not imaging them. Everyone is linked, through more than just blood. We are all digitally linked, be that through messages or images. I look up at the old guy, I smile. He must have been around when letters were still a thing.

"Use it to your advantage I always say, don't let it use you!" he laughed, taking out his phone. His digital lines scattered around, connecting with many people in the area; one of the people being me. To my surprise, the man stood and shook my hand "I am here to talk about your muffin recipes".

It is happening. Something my mother could never do. She had tried for years, marketing in the town, selling on special holidays just to get her treats to the world. Although she did an amazing job, she could never get out of the town. She was always baking from her kitchen. Today, with a few years of blogging and thousands of photos virally spread around the internet. I had the confidence to send a singular email. I had written it before sitting down to have lunch. Because of it, I was now in the presence of someone who could change my life.

"Are you ready to go big with these ideas, set up your own shop?" he questioned.

"Of course" I answer without a second thought. My dream came true because I embraced the world I lived within. I took advantage of what was in front of me, never letting it take advantage of me.

J. M. Robbins

OPTOMETRY
DIGITAL OPTOMETRY

The digitisation of our daily life is no longer astonishing. It became an irreversible fact long ago. Nowadays changing **reading habits** and the **increasing amount of time spent on PCs and smartphones** cause new challenges to vision.

Therefore, the demand for optometric services is constantly on the rise. Of course, digitalisation also finds its way to Optometry. Every new device or machine contains digital components and engenders a faster, more secure and more precise measurement and fabrication. Opticians and optometrists offer a wide variety of refraction and optometric services.

We can take measurements with the most amazing equipment, and something that has really impressed me is the easyScan. EasyScan employs Scanning Laser Ophthalmoscope (SLO) technology for superior imaging. Retinopathies become more easily detectable with a clear and sharp image for accurate diagnosis. Best of all, we can email the images and the patient can share the experience with friends.

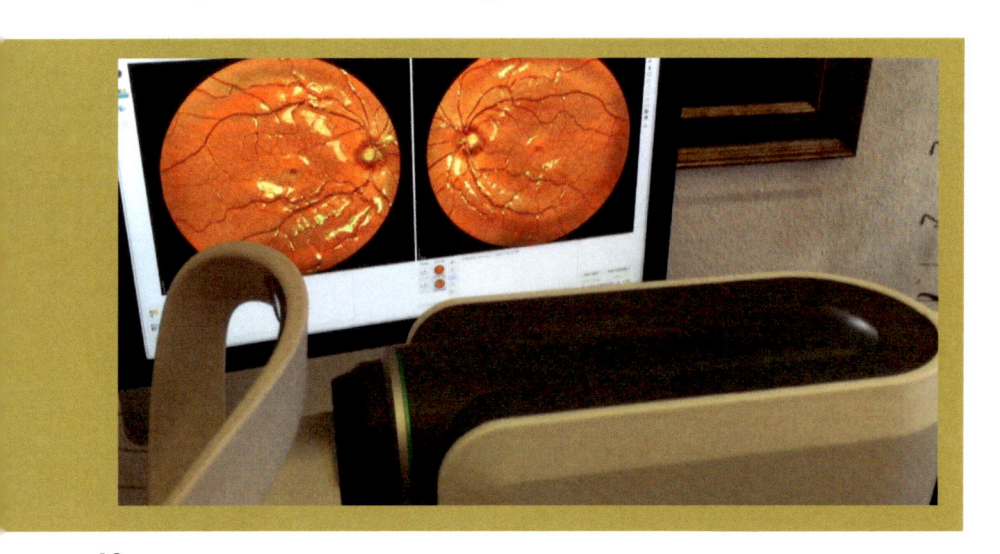

> **LEARN WHAT IT TAKES TO BUILD A BRAND AND ESTABLISH YOURSELF IN TODAY'S EVER-CHANGING, DIGITAL WORLD VIA @GARYVEE #ASKGARYVEE**

TIPS FOR HEALTHY EYES

EAT FOR GOOD VISION

Regularly eating food with nutrients like omega-3 fatty acids, lutein, zinc and vitamins C and E may help fight problems like macular degeneration.

Example of Infographic

QUIT SMOKING

Smoking increases the risk of getting optic nerve damage and macular degeneration.

WEAR SUNGLASSES

Too much UV exposure makes you more likely to get macular degeneration. Choose sunglasses that block 99% to 100% of both UVA and UVB rays

PROTECT EYEWEAR

Use safety eyewear at home, at work, and while playing sports. If you work with hazardous or airborne materials, wear safety glasses every time.

TAKE A BREAK FROM SCREENS

Staring at a computer screen can cause eyestrain, blurry vision and much more.

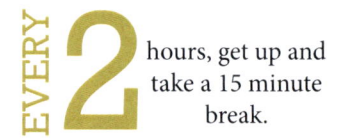

EVERY 2 hours, get up and take a 15 minute break.

FACEBOOK

Facebook is an online social networking service headquartered in Menlo Park, California. Its website was launched on 4 February, 2004, by Mark Zuckerberg with his Harvard College roommates and fellow students Eduardo Saverin, Andrew McCollum, Dustin Moskovitz and Chris Hughes.
- Wikipedia

After registering to Facebook, users can create a profile (this is different to a business page), add other users as "friends", send messages, update their status, add photos, share videos and receive notifications. Additionally, users may join common-interest user groups.
Did you know that 'ABDO' have a group?

You're probably thinking "Why does my business needs to be on Facebook?"

With Facebook, your business can reach millions of people, target exactly the demographic you wish and have direct communication with your customers.
A Business Page looks a little different from a Personal Page - this is where you gain 'Fans' instead of 'Friends'. Advertising from your personal page can end with your account being suspended for not following Facebook's rules - trust me it happens!

To create a Business Page (also known as a Fan Page) you simply need to:
Click Arrow in Top Right Corner of your Page > Click Create Page > Fill in your Business Details

After this has been completed you can start building your brand. Make sure all the graphics you are using match your other online channels. Make your website, Facebook, Twitter, Youtube, and others look the same. You want to create a unifying theme! Pick a suitable display picture and cover photo, fill out the 'About' section so everything is completed.

Once you add an address, your customers can start leaving you Facebook reviews. Now let's get posting! When posting an update to Facebook, make sure your post is either engaging, entertaining or informative. If it's none of these - don't post! You want to give your customers value, so give them some tips on what to do when their glasses break, or show them some pictures of that new range that has just come in.

When creating a Facebook business strategy, it's important to think through what you want to achieve. Is your goal to drive traffic to your website? Do you want customers to call your practice? Just make sure you are clear of your primary reasons for being on Facebook before you start working on it.

One of the biggest benefits of having a Business Page is your Insights. These are Facebook's version of analytics. You can find out how well you are doing this week in terms of new likes, reach, what time your fans are online and more. The Insights appear at the top of the page just above your cover photo.

> Asking a question at the end of your post yields a 100% increase in comments over posts with a question in the middle of the post.

FACEBOOK GROUPS

Facebook Groups can only be joined from a personal account, and you can join 6000 of them - if you really want to. This means you can't be part of a group via your business page. There are many different aims of a group, so make sure you are joining the right groups for the right reasons.

Some groups may be area specific eg 'We Love London' or 'Goodlooking Happy People Enfield'. 'We Love London' is a Facebook group where people in London can share stories about things to do and what's happening in their local area. There are also groups which buy and sell products and goods, groups where people advertise their company and private groups where you can catch up with old friends.

Here is where you can put your marketing hat on - create or join a group where you can advertise your practice for free. This could be a group dedicated to your local area. A lot of groups on Facebook aren't monetised, so take advantage of this while it lasts.

FACEBOOK STATS

Demo and Geo Targeting

Target by: Country, City or Postcode

Workplace & Education Targeting

Target by: Gender, Age, Birthday, Relationship Status, Language, Workplace and Education

Likes and Interest Targeting

Target by: Favourite TV shows, Movies, Books, Music, Hobbies, Religion, Political Views

SMALL NUMBER OF TARGETED USERS

There are more than 2 million active advertisers on Facebook. That means advertising is more consistent and competitive than ever, and ads with high quality content and appeal will rise to the top!

QUICK FACEBOOK WINS

7 Easy Steps to Facebook Success

1. Join groups in your area

2. Spend £5.00 a week on adverts

3. Always upload more then 2 pictures

4. Use the @ to get engagement

5. Learn from Mari Smith

6. Remember the Purpose of Your Page. Never lose sight of why you created your page. Create a bond between you, your brand, traffic to your website. Educate, Entertain and Engage

7.
ENGAGEMENT

TALK LIKE YOU WOULD TO A NEIGHBOUR OR BEST FRIEND

FACEBOOK ADVERTISING

Facebook advertising is like word-of-mouth marketing on steroids. There are different stages to the adverts and you don't have to spend your whole marketing budget to get a result. Using the 'Boost a Post' option is the easiest advert to use. It appears under your post after your page has successfully gained 100 Likes. The minimum spend to boost a post is £1 per day. You can specify who you would like your advert to be shown to; you can pick the age range, location and interests. After your advert has finished, you will gain insights on how well your advert did.

Next we have 'Adverts Manager'. This is a more advanced version of 'Boost a Post'. You have the opportunity to be more specific. You can also split-test your adverts in the 'Ad Set' (split-testing is similar to blind testing with a placebo). You can pick which outcome you would like for the advert. This could be to gain more likes, reach more local people, website conversions and more. Make sure you pick the right outcome. Your advert is not guaranteed to be approved. Facebook have their own guidelines

> There are more advanced adverts available - but that's another book for another day!

which you will need to follow in order to deliver a kick-ass advert that will bring in some money.

This way of using Facebook for business advertising has proven to be very successful for countless companies. When you do it, you'll get the results right away. Just compare how much you spend on Facebook ads to the revenue, and you'll know whether or not you need to tweak your campaign in any way. It's a great opportunity for your company to make

BE THE EXPERT!

FACEBOOK LIVE

FACEBOOK LIVE IS A GAME CHANGER!

Being able to ENGAGE with your online network in real time is an amazing way to promote and interact with your customers. As already mentioned in this book ENGAGMENT is key in any buisness and this is the number one best way to do just that!

1. Tell people when you're broadcasting. This will help build antisipation.

2. Go Live when you have a strong connection.

3. Write a catchy description before going Live.

4. Ask viewers to subscribe to your Live notifications.

5. Say hello to your commenters by name and respond to their comments Live. Your audience will be thrilled to hear you mentioned their name.

6. Broadcast for longer period of time to reach more people.

Viewers of your video can share and comment, making going live a new crazy experience. So pick up your phone, get on the Facebook app and click the little red Live button. It will open up new connects for your business that you didn't think you could have with just a smile and click of a button.

FACEBOOK CASE STUDY

Humanising your brand is one of the best ways to receive interaction from your customers. Forever putting out content and calls to action alone, simply doesn't work.

One day, someone came in to Goodlooking Optics and said, "you remind me of Scott Disick!" For those of you who don't know, Scott is from the TV show "Keeping up with the Kardashians". Like anyone, I was happy to be compared with a celebrity and, so we thought we could integrate it offline and online and ask the rest of our customers if they agreed. What we did was to get a picture of Scott Disick and then a picture of me and put them next to each other. No fancy Photoshop business, just a simple

goodlooking optics with Garry Kousoulou at goodlooking optics.
4 November 2013

Garry got compared to Scott Disick from 'Keeping Up With The Kardashians' this morning. What do you think - could Garry be a Kardashian?

As you can see, a simple post using real people can get you real results. We received 61 Likes, 28 Comments, and a reach of 1,391 people organically! With simple tips, such as tagging the right people and putting a location in the post, you can out-smart the Facebook boffins that only want around 8% of your fans to see your post! You don't always need to pay to get results.

Here are some tips to get more likes, more eyeballs to see your posts, more engagement, and more money!

■ A picture is proven to attract more people –
but don't always stick to a pic! Experiment with links, simple status updates, and videos.

■ Always encourage engagement
This could be a call to action, asking your fans a question and asking for their opinion.

■ Involve your friends
If you've got friends or family around, ask them if they can invite all their friends to Like your page. Around 10-20% of people will accept Like requests, so if your niece has 500 friends on Facebook, you're likely to get at least 50 new Likes. What is there to lose?

■ Encourage fans to share your post
Sharing goes out to 100% of the friends of the person who shared your post. So, if the "sharer" has 750 friends, guess how many people have just seen your post?

■ Return the favour
If someone comments on your page, don't just like their comment, comment saying thank you. Your page gets rated on your response time, as well as a lot of other things.

■ Use a milestone!
Using a 'Milestone' is a quick and easy way for up to 100% of your fans to see what you're celebrating. Good Looking Optics recently had its 10,000th customer come through the doors, so we took a picture of them with a prize, uploaded it to Facebook and made it a Milestone.

These rule are the same for changing your cover photo.

Happy Facebooking
- we wish you all the success!

TWITTER

BY SUJAN SHAH

CARRIER BAG SHOP

I was in charge of the social media used to promote Gary Vaynerchuk's "Vaynerworld" tour. We were mainly promoting his recent book launch and were able to use social media heavily as this event was targeted at people who were social media savvy and interested in social media itself.

Who is my audience?

I could promote the hell out of an event but this could easily fail if I targeted the wrong people.

With all social networks now, they have a massive amount of data so you can accurately target someone. Some social media requires being "friends" with someone to interact with them but Twitter allows anyone to be targeted.

With "Vaynerworld" we utilised keywords related to social media, marketing, growing business etc. and it was easy to find the right people by using Twitter algorithms.

This is the same tactic we use within Carrier Bag Shop. Anyone and any company can be targeted through Twitter.

Naturally, Twitter is more effective for some than others. You don't necessarily need to use direct links. For example, with Carrier Bag Shop, we don't need to target specific "carrier bag interested" people, there's always something else that people are interested in. Paths aren't always linear and should be mixed up occasionally to keep interest.

24

CASE STUDIES

Twitter
All conversations are visible – give your user-base things that they want to share with people.

Vaynerworld
Fans behave differently to regular audiences and are generally better as they will pay more and expect less, plus they're more likely to share content. By utilising the fans, we were able to boost our presence on days such as Gary Vaynerchuk's birthday where we utilised the hashtag #seeyouatvaynerworld, and 18-20% of his followers began retweeting with this hashtag.

Hashtags are now less powerful. In B2B, the hashtag has to be relevant for your community, not to go global. Very few businesses are able to make hashtags go viral. Is the hashtag viable as something your community will want to search for?
Twitter has tools that make life easier. You shouldn't blindly follow people as this isn't very effective and it's easy to hit limits with few results.

What is effective, is targeting groups of people who have similar interests and are on Twitter; and you can create a list/group for your own use. This way you can keep these people in one place where you can instantly reach them.

Vaynerworld Tweets
We were lucky to be able to piggyback off Gary's fame and followers.

We had 667 followers at the time, but since the event it has to dropped off a little, which is natural.

There are still videos and pictures there to be seen. It's important to keep engaging followers even if nothing is currently planned for the future.

Sujan Shah (right)
Gary Vaynerchuk (left)
Sujan Shah

TWITTER TIP

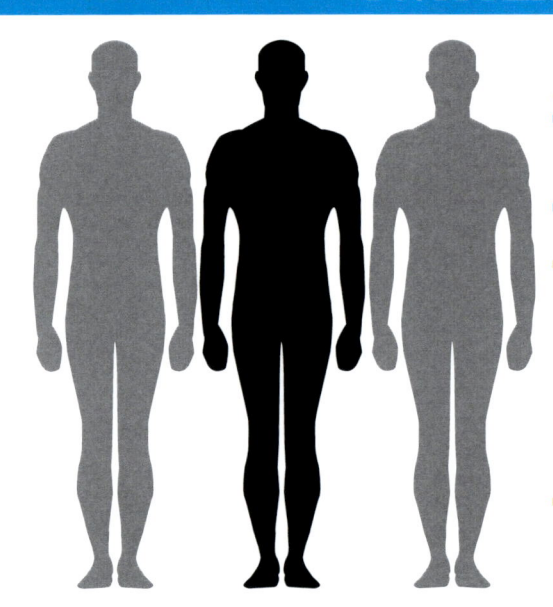

Top Tips for Twitter

Follow 3 and 1 will follow you back

On average every 10th follower goes to your website

■ Interaction With Audience

Interacting with your audience improves your company's credibility

■ Don't Buy Followers

Buying Twitter followers doesn't get you an audience and won't improve your company's stature

■ Hold Regular Competitions

Holding regular competitions attracts more business

■ Business and Personal

It's key to remember the difference between Business and Personal

■ Follow Friday

Using #FollowFriday to promote others can lead them to returning the favour for you

- Got new stock in? Tweet about new frames, cases etc. Keep your customers informed and engaged!

- Suggest a solution to a problem that someone has posted. You could link it to a web tutorial.

- Don't be a secret agent - add your twitter name to your website, business cards, emails, and signatures. Let people find you!

- Offer a special promotion or discount to your followers and ask for retweets. This can get more followers and website visits.

- More followers means more reach for your tweets. Use the search function, find people in your niche, follow and start conversations.

- Don't send every tweet to Facebook - the two platforms are different and need a different approach.

- Treat social media like a networking event. Nobody listens to the person who walks in and starts selling.

- To prevent problems, always set up and implement a clear social media policy for your employees.

- Include an @ mention if you're referencing a thought leader in your niche - give them an incentive to retweet.

- **Aim for tweet lengths of 120-130 character; don't use up all 140. Allow space for Retweets with comments.**

- **Position yourself as an expert by producing free, informative content and answering questions.**

- **Looking to hire someone? The majority of companies (>80%) now use social media as part of their recruitment.**

- **Don't sit back and let everyone else tweet, jump in on a conversation, offer help, build your community and earn trust.**

- **Don't post links with no explanation of what they're about.**

- **A tweet has a very short life span. Approx 90% of engagement happens within the first hour of tweeting.**

- **Make sure you have an RSS button on your website/blog so that visitors can easily subscribe to updates. No need to be shy ;)**

- **Fill out your bio using the max. 160 characters. Who are you and what do you do? Include website link and a good headshot/logo.**

- **Don't tweet in text-speak - be creative and make best use of 140 characters. Remember to leave a few for Retweets.**

- **The ideal time to get retweeted is around 4pm EST (9pm GMT) on a Friday.**

YOUTUBE

Videos are quite possibly the main relationship marketing accelerator; therefore online video platforms such as YouTube are at the fore of getting your message out to the majority. Utilising a video is such a great way of spreading the message that you want to deliver, and it's certainly one of my favourites.

The shelf life of a video is fantastic. A Tweet could last all of 12 seconds but a video can last for a decade or more until it is removed. During this period – with the correct promotion – these videos can go to work for you, communicating to your audiences and raising your online profile and presence.

As far as online communication goes, videos are great! They let people see who you are and what you're about, and this helps them to relate to you and be more inclined to want to do business with you. Now even the audio from videos on YouTube is helping your SEO, as Google listens to the words used within the video and these can count towards your keywords.

It's easy to become an expert with videos after just a short time. This is great as viewers can tell when you have that little bit of experience and gravitas and it makes them trust you more. Videos are also a really good online tool for going viral. The right video can reach millions of people all around the world these days, and can get everyone talking about you. Perhaps best of all, these videos can be really cheap to produce.

Over 4 billion videos are viewed each day.

Over 800 million unique users (first time users) visit YouTube each month.

Once a video is made, the description and the tag are vitally important. YouTube is the second biggest search engine in the world, so using the right words can really increase your rankings. For example, if you search for the perfect baked potato on Google, it'll give you blogs and videos along with the links to webpages. Google puts videos at the top of their search results due to their effectiveness, as a simple two minute video of something can give you a much better idea of it than a bit of text that takes you two minutes to read.

SEO can be utilised by peppering search engine buzzwords in the right places. Don't just repeat them in places where they don't fit. This includes your tags, though don't overdo these. There's also the possible guerrilla tactic of including misspelled tags, as typos are common when searching online, and this will catch those misspelled searches too.

Technically, by setting up a YouTube page you're creating a tv channel. This is the channel to use to broadcast to your viewers whenever they want to view it. I hasten to add that there should be brand unity with this channel, alongside everything else you do, in terms of brand/colour/feel.

From my own experience, customers have travelled long distances just because they've seen a video of me. They were so impressed with the sincerity and integrity within it, that they wanted to buy from me. Let's face it, nobody can act like an Oscar nominated actor straight away, it's difficult to really fake a video. So when your video is sincere and the passion shows, people will trust you.

Top tips about how to set up your YouTube layout

Engaging Video

Video should be findable

Title tag and description

Brand your channel

Add annotations

Add your channel art

Your channel trailer

TOP VIDEO TIPS

- Think big, start small
- Get support - watch YouTube for what you are unsure about
- Start with one platform at a time if you're not comfortable with social media
- Answer as many comments as you can immediately
- Comment on the videos of others, as long as they are valid comments
- Have fun with it and don't be frightened
- See if others are doing what you plan to do and see if you can do it differently whilst learning from them
- Post regularly. If you say that you'll do a video on a Friday – do it. On YouTube you can queue videos for when you're away
- Think of who your audience is and how you address them. Have a vision of who they are. When I'm doing videos for employers, I envision a man in his forties who owns a small business in the Midlands. With job seekers I imagine a room full of 16-18 year-olds, eager to learn.
- Don't do it in fits and spurts. The ability to schedule videos is so important. Google wants to see consistency.

> Hours of videos watch per month on Youtube 6 Billion.

- **Get opinions from your audience, not those who are close to you. However, in my case my own children's opinions are relevant as they are both in my demographic and think that I'm uncool!**
- **Keep a consistent brand/style.**
- **Don't try to be "hip" if you're of a certain age… People see through it.**
- **If recording in the same place consistently, create a mini studio.**
- **Don't regurgitate material on separate platforms as it's lazy and each platform is different.**
- **You're not going to please everyone, so don't try to.**
- **Don't be frightened of sticking to your values and beliefs. Don't be bland.**
- **Don't be afraid of occasional long content.**

> You can learn to do anything through watching Youtube! Become the expert!

YOUTUBE CASE STUDY
BY GRAHAM MARTIN

Orchard Recruitment
SETTING UP A YOUTUBE CHANNEL

Graham set up a YouTube channel three years ago, using a professional videography company.

Initially he filmed in a boardroom. He would sweat profusely and was very nervous.

Now he has two series of approximately 16 videos per series, to help employers to recruit people.

After about 10 videos he was on a roll. The camera guys gave him a good pre-production pep talk that gave him confidence.

He eventually went out into the field to his clients. These videos had less style than the others but he was more at ease with them, which gave him added confidence due to the more relaxed surroundings.

Now he has the confidence to shoot his own videos with a HD flip-cam. His former camera guys taught him and encouraged him to go it alone with what he had learnt.

> **USE MAILCHIMP TO HELP CONNECT TO YOUR AUDIENCE**

Some of his videos were planned and some were simply off the hoof, as it were.

Then he started using Twitter. You need people supporting and encouraging you, especially to tell you when you're no good! Even so, keep trying until you get it right. Then strive to make it better!

The cost of this is a simple flip-cam which you can get secondhand on eBay. There's no excuse not to have one or more. I certainly recommend it!

4 YOUTUBE MUST DO'S

Professional and nonprofessional support

In his first year Graham had a huge amount of input from professional video guys. Without them it wouldn't have happened. For the last two years he has worked by himself, plus his support base. People who are going it alone should look for others to work with, to help them to get going.

Average length of videos

Aim for under five minutes using specific themes. Give your audience time to mature – around six months – and they'll let you know what they want to see.

Engage

Respond to every email and comment. Make it easy for your audience to comment by putting email and website links on your videos. Use tags and descriptions that apply to them. As an example, suppose you're a motor racing fan and create videos about that. If you were to add a tag such as "Alonso's facial hair", you may find a niche audience for yourself.

What would you want to see in a video and how would you want to be responded to? Niche and special interest audiences are where you want to be, and they're much easier to interact with.

An ego's all well and good, but this sort of thing is far too time-consuming for that.
Be aware of changes to technology and be prepared to change with it if need be.
Beware of false Gods! Too many people proclaim to be social media experts.

How to keep content fresh

Build up ideas in a folder. Always keep a flip-cam close to hand in case an idea strikes.

INSTAGRAM

Instagram was created to tell a story with images. We are going to teach you how to use Instagram effectively in optics!

Our Top Three Tips

- **Connect your Facebook account**
- **Use relevant, popular hashtags**
- **Engage by following others and liking their pages**

Pick a great picture and make sure it isn't blurry! Although Instagram has a 'sharpening' function, it isn't magic. For an example see figure 1.

The best examples are pictures of frames, patient's trying on your frames, before and after shots and work-related activities. Silver Linings Opticians do this very well. For an example see figure 2.

Figure 1

Figure 2

What hashtag should I use?

The top two Instagram hashtags for opticians are:

#EYEWEAR & #SUNGLASSES

SIMPLE STEPS TO SUCCESS

■ 1. Upload a picture / video

■ 2. Minimum Five # per photo

■ 3. Post Consistently

#Adidas. #Sunglasses #Exclusive

This is all you need for a perfect Instagram post. Nice and easy.

Perfect Instagram Image... This nearly broke the internet!

A GoodLooking Optics trip to the #Optical show in Munich.

There's no point in having a huge social media presence if you cannot provide a world class service.

Remember - everything you do online is amplified.

Lucy Hall, Nigel Boterill, Garry Kousoulou in 2006.
My favourite Nigel saying is
"Don't become world class at getting ready."

www.slideshare.net/goodlookingoptics/the-15-customer-service-commandments

MARKETING

OFFLINE MARKETING

A Shark's Tale, a 21st Dilemma.
ONLINE OR OFFLINE NETWORKING?

When I was a young lad, my wise old dad shared a business saying with me that has stayed with me a lifetime......"Son it's not the sharks that swim in the sea that you should fear, it's the ones that operate outside the sea you should fear most!"

So for me the million dollar question became, who is it safe to do business with and how do I go about it?

The general consensus amongst the 'baby boomer' generation is "it's not what you know, it's who you know", it's jobs for the boys. So go seek those right people to mingle with and if you're lucky you might get on!

Going forward, attitudes changed for generation X. They saw the advent of fair play and equal rights for all, an equal playing field.

Today we have generation Y and the Millennials (Z). The 21st century has seen an online revolution! Business, social, dating, gaming, everything lives in a virtual online world. Who you can meet in business, and in life, has become infinite.

The worrying problem is that there is no depth; a lot of it is superficial. Appearances can be just profile deep. Appearances can be photoshopped. Business relationships can be marketed in an appealing way and hide that worrying shark fin that will get you!

We are living in, and witnessing, an era with two different skills which are poles apart. Online skills and offline skills. Both have their benefits, both have their pitfalls.

This brings us to how we are as individuals. Generally, people do business with people they like, know and trust.

We often say in a personal relationship once you like someone, it's good to live together, to get to know your partner. Yep getting to know someone makes sense. If you like someone and get to know them, who knows what could be possible! Revolutionary idea! However in business one wouldn't suggest living with someone before you do business with them!

So how about this as an idea.... Once a week spend what would normally be dead time informally getting to know some local business professionals. Discuss business and find out how to help each other. Share contacts and recommend each other. Now there's a weird concept; help others in business rather than eating them alive!

Well after informally getting to know each other, how about running a structured business meeting designed to help each other get business. We could individually share what we are looking for and take minutes. What if we then decided to help others, yep that weird concept again. It's been proven that one's personal happiness revolves around how much you help others. If we practice this in our personal life, why not in our business life?

Well what I described is the concept of BNI; that's Business Network International, a 31 year-old business referral organisation. It has a proven structure where reliable honest business

> Therefore, it's key that whatever you do, whether on or off line, it is in a structured environment and that one compliments the other.

people meet weekly to create long-lasting relationships that lead to business. How? By helping other like-minded business people.

The online digital age is fantastic for touching people we would not normally touch. But we are human and not totally digital. I guess face-to-face people relationship skills is something my generation could and should share with our digital online Millennials, and I'm sure the younger gurus are more than happy to share their digital online know-how.

Balance in most things is often a great yard stick…whoops should I have said metre stick?!

First you need to like what you see, whether online or face-to-face. Once you like what you see, you need to get to know someone and build up trust, then a fruitful business relationship can ensue.

Online is brilliant for making those initial introductions but nothing can beat a face-to-face meeting, where you can experience all the things that make a person tick.

The million dollar answer is to surround yourself with those that you have got to know and trust over a period of time. That's people who have a proven track record as ethical business people. In his book "Losing my Virginity" Richard Branson put his success down to surrounding himself with people who are better than him!

Which brings me back to where we started. My wise old dad's words "A shark in the sea in its environment is unlikely to harm anyone and is nowhere near as dangerous as rogue business people in an unstructured environment!".

BNI

Tim Nicolaou
BNI Executive Director
London North East
"Making a difference to local people's lives and business communities"

EMAIL MARKETING

MailChimp

EMAIL 2500 PEOPLE FOR FREE

A range of templates for you to change and use for your company.

WHY SHOULD I USE MAILCHIMP?

Sending mass email to people without having an unsubscribe button is classed as an unsolicited email. Not having someone's permission to email them is also considered unsolicited.

If someone hands you a business card, feel free to add them to your own unique MailChimp List.

And create different lists and send different information

IT'S AS SIMPLE AS 1. 2. 3!

Other alternatives to you CRM are Constant Contact and Sales Force. FACT: When you do a mail shot you will always see a jump in your web traffic.

Little Tip: the subject line is more crucial then the content. It totally effects the open rate is you get the subject line wrong.

THREE TYPES OF DIGITAL MARKETING

INTERRUPTION MARKETING

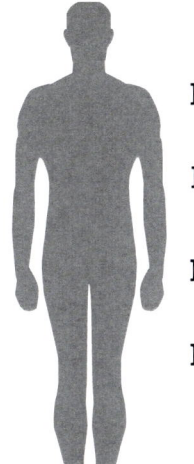

FACEBOOK ADS

BANNERS

POP UPS

PPC

Interruption Marketing is the traditional model of product promotion, in which people have to stop what they're doing to pay attention to the marketing message or deal with it in some other way. This method can irritate potential customers if mass used. Examples of interrupt marketing include: telemarketing calls and mail campaigns.

RETURN ON INVESMENT ⭐

RELATIONSHIP MARKETING

The way people discover content on social media differs from the way they do so through search engines ie, Google.

On social media, people are not looking for anything in particular. They want to be entertained by the people, brands, magazines, publishers, etc. that they follow. When they need a service or product they will buy when they need. It builds your brand and loyalty. Key to success. Give. When the person needs you it will happen.

LINKEDIN

FACEBOOK

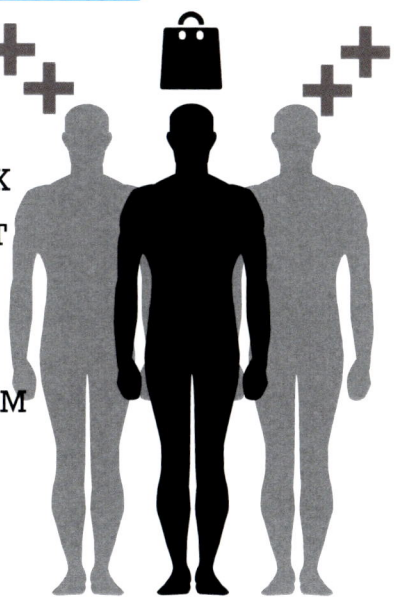

SNAPCHAT

TWITTER

PINTREST

INSTAGRAM

YOUTUBE

EMAIL

RETURN ON INVESMENT ⭐⭐⭐

SEARCH MARKETING

Search Marketing is the process of gaining traffic and visibility from search engines like google or bing through both paided and unpaid efforts. Using 'SEO' short for search engine optimisation can help your earnings by bring in more traffic through unpaid or free listings. SEO works in the same way that usings '#' hashtags on instgram or twitter does. Using spesific words upon your websites or blogs can up your profile on search engines.

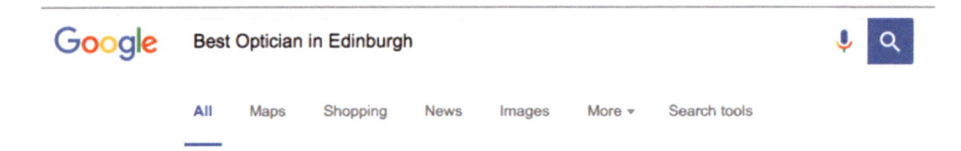

Google | Best Optician in Edinburgh

All   Maps   Shopping   News   Images   More ▾   Search tools

For example, when you looking for somewhere to get you hair cut or you want your eyes tested, your going to be looking for the 'BEST' place to do that.

Typing into Google 'best opticians in Enfield' or 'best sight test in Edinburgh' the top organic result will probably get the phone call. All you have to do on your website or blog is these tags. When discribing your company and what you do, put that your the best place in Enfield to get your eyes tested.

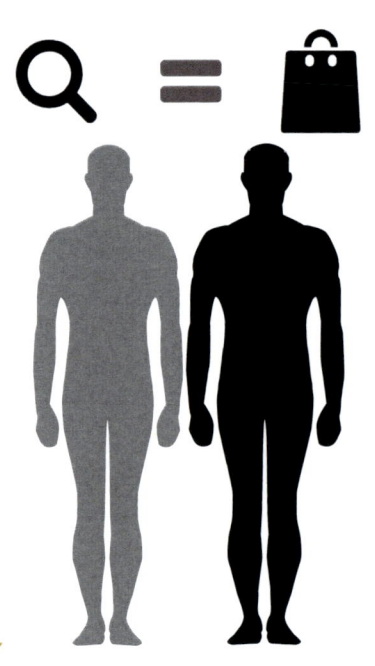

RETURN ON INVESMENT

★★★★★

GOODLOOKING: CASE STUDY

Goodlooking optics have a unified coordinated approach to their digital marketing. Connected all the digital dots, with the website and collecting email address being the main focus.

Vital Statistics

Website
1.7k Searches every 30 days
30 people request directions
Average 57 visits a day
1.34 sec Average Stay
Page one ranking for over 1,000 words
Bounce rate 72
52 local reviews
All social media platforms linked to website
50 calls a week from mobile site to practice number
registered on over 1,000 directories
WooRank 76

Youtube
500 videos with over 1.5 million views
1 new video a week

Instagram
2 new pictures a week
333 posts

Twitter
21,000 followers
Member of 130 lists
Follow a min of 100 local people a week

Facebook
2,852 Fans on the business page
683 check ins
72% response rate
Average response time 15 minutes
Community group 15,036
Average spend on adverts a week $15.00
20 5 star reviews
3 Facebook lives a week
Aim for 2 checkins a week
Likalizer Score 72

Linkedin
7,000 connections
Average 200 people look at the profile
680 average views on the blog
members of 50 groups

Email
8,000 email address. Mail chimp once a month to everybody

Blog
Over 100 blogs that have been indexed with Google though our WordPress site.
One 500 word blog every 4 weeks with video.

BRANDING

Read this chapter carefully. Get this bit wrong and
EFFECTIVENESS IS LOST!

I should begin by explaining why the book begins with a chapter about branding and marketing. You need to be crystal clear about the message that you want your business to amplify and the story you want it to tell. Without stating the obvious, put out the right consistent message to get the results you want.

Just before opening my optical practice in 2004 I was obsessed. I was obsessed with reading, obsessed with how I was NOT going to fail. This educational journey began by learning how to market and brand a business. A business has three departments: finance, operations, and marketing. Right off the bat I already had a natural interest in marketing, I found all the books about marketing that applied to me and every one that I read was mentally devoured.

Let me explain to you the purpose of marketing as I see it. The aim of marketing is to continue getting new customers whilst also keeping the existing ones sweet. Marketing is how you present your brand, be it a personal brand or that of your business. Your brand is what you wear on your sleeve, complete with the core values that it represents. This is what your customers trust. So obviously, creating such a thing out of the blue is not easy.

Out of all the books I read, one was a stand out that made a lot of sense to me. It was a little yellow book. I lent it to someone and don't remember the title, but it must have been good if they didn't return it! But let me share the content with you.

The concept is easy - name three of your favourite brands and explain why you chose those brands. Here were my three at the time:

Singapore Airlines. They had amazing customer service. I was on a flight back from Australia at ridiculous o'clock and the cabin crew still had warming smiles and wanted to help us as much as possible. I have never experienced such great customer service before or since.

MTV. I love music and back then MTV played the best and the coolest music around.

Tesco. You could buy the best brands and the value range all under one roof. They catered for the needs of everyone who walked into their store.

I wanted my opticians, GoodLooking Optics, to encompass all the values of these companies and brands that I love. Your favourite brands should help encapsulate what your business should feel like. What do their mission statements say about them and how can you replicate those thoughts into your own business? Everything that you do should be based on these key values and everything should be tied together by one common thing – your brand. None of your marketing material should stray even an inch from your branding and key values, be it business cards, leaflets or websites. If it doesn't tie in with the brand - scrap it!

I tried this exercise on a singer who was struggling to brand herself. The technique worked just as well. She chose Amy Winehouse, Michael Jackson, and Aretha Franklin. After she gave me these names we were then able to look at how these artists got their breaks, how they styled themselves and their albums and how we could learn from these to better her future. This worked just as well and she is now moving forward in her music career.

My advice is to list your top three brands and look at the companies' mission statements online. You can really get a lot of inspiration from them. Before long other companies will want to follow you and learn from your brand.

Apple's first mission statement was "to make a contribution to the world by making tools for the mind that advance humankind." It's a lot easier to amplify your message when you know your brand and you're comfortable with it.

In conclusion, if you are trying to build a brand, stick to three characteristics of the brand you are trying to mimic, whether it be online or offline, for example business cards, YouTube and Facebook.

5 TOP TIPS
FOR SUCCESSFULLY
Branding
YOUR OPTICIANS

1. IMPORTANCE OF A LOGO

Your logo appears on ALL your business marketing. So it is imperative that it reflects your business as you intend it to. A logo should be simple and adaptable. Ask yourself these important questions:

Is your logo scalable without the loss of any quality?
Does your logo work across a variety of media e.g. digitally, in print etc.?
Do you own the original PDF file?

If not, speak with your designer today.

2. CONSISTENCY OF BRAND IDENTITY

Consistent brand identity reinforces your values. How do we know which element of your marketing clients will come in to contact with first? Will it be your business card or your website perhaps?

This explains why consistency across all your business platforms and literature needs to be considered and worked on. Is your business identity in each of these areas of marketing consistent?...

- ❏ Business Card
- ❏ Letterhead
- ❏ Compliment Slip
- ❏ Website
- ❏ Facebook Profile
- ❏ Twitter Profile
- ❏ Shop Fascia
- ❏ Leaflets
- ❏ Vehicle Graphics
- ❏ Publication Advert
- ❏ Email Marketing
- ❏ Loyalty Cards

3.

USE DIFFERENT MEDIA

To get the most out of your marketing appealing to a variety of demographics in the most effective way is key - e.g. Social Media may appeal to ages 18-45 but be less effective to those over 60.

Always have your audience in mind - age, gender, location, profession etc. Explore campaigns through different media such as Print, Direct Mail, Social Media, Websites, Window Graphics, Vehicle Graphics etc. to see what proves most effective for your client base and for your return on investment.

4.

USE PROFESSIONAL IMAGES

You will be amazed at the difference professionally produced images can make to your marketing. Original photography is always best but if you don't have the budget to hire a photographer, use professional stock images until you do!

5.

INVOLVE A PROFESSIONAL

Do-It-Yourself branding may be tempting but works out costly in the long run! It will take up your valuable time, money and the results will not be what you envisaged. You will have to review this at a later date as your business starts to grow, regardless. You also run the risk of jeopardising your image and trust from your clients. Don't do it!

Creative Agencies provide fresh, innovative ideas that give your brand the right footing to aid business growth from the start. It may add an extra cost to start with, but will prove to be an invaluable investment.

For more advice and tips for your business, contact us today!

07949 320 486

georgia@marshmallowdesign.co.uk
www.marshmallowdesign.co.uk

marshmallow

10 Year Logo Design
GoodLooking Optics

CELEBRATING 10 YEARS
EST. SINCE 2004

WHY DO YOU NEED A WEBSITE?

BY PAZBI ZAVATZKI

You might be thinking that your Opticians has plenty of customers, lots of referrals from word of mouth and there is no need for a website. Heck you might already have a Facebook page so you are thinking I'm already online. You'd be wrong and here is why.

Imagine there is a person who recently moved to your area. They don't know anyone but their eyes need to be tested, they open up Chrome or Google Maps on their phone and search for "Optician near me" the search engine checks their location and populates a list. They click and call the one with the best reviews or maybe the one that's nearest. But what they definitely don't do is call yours because you aren't on the list. Not having a website is the same as having your shutters down for every single Mobile user in your area who doesn't already know you.

This is all due to the way search engines such as Google, Yahoo and Bing crawl the internet. When you exclusively use social media accounts for your online presence not only are you depending on those platforms to work but you miss out on a wealth of customisation, seo opportunities and branding. Having a website is similar to owning your own shop that you can customise however you like and sell whatever you want, whereas having a page on a social media platform is the equivalent of an ad on the corkboard of the newsagent.

How do I set it up?

Creating a website first requires planning. Decide the features your website will have, such as a blog (highly recommended), e-commerce functionality (if you want to sell online) or even booking systems.

Once you have your goal for the site, a design can be put together that is consistent with your branding and then developed into a working website. A very important tip for working with developers, you should always buy your domain name yourself and register it under your real information. Afterwards the developer can manage the domain and hosting but at least if there are any problems you can't be tied down or blackmailed because you control the domain.

Regardless of what type of website you have built, most people when searching for an optician are usually interested in 3 things, where are you, when are you open and how can I book an appointment, there are a few key things you need for any homepage:

1. Keep it simple - Don't overcrowd the website with too much information, just the important stuff.

2. Make it easy to contact you - People have short attention spans and if they can't find a contact number or email within 30 seconds they will get annoyed and find an alternative. Also make the numbers / emails as links they can click and automatically call or email you.

3. Post your opening times - By posting clear opening times you can save potential customers time and your receptionist from having to answer tedious phone calls. This information will also be collated into your Google+ page.

4. Add your address - Although embedding maps look great you should always add the address in text so that it can get picked up by the search engine spiders.

5. Ask a professional for help - Although you can build your own site, you may find you are wasting time learning how to customise it the way it you like. Hiring a professional will give you a outstanding website without the hassle. Saving you time, money and stress.

WEB DESIGN & DEVELOPMENT
GRAPHIC DESIGN & BRANDING
APP DESIGN & DEVELOPMENT
SEO CONSULTING
COPYWRITING
TRAINING & BUSINESS CONSULTING

SOME TALENTED PEOPLE.COM

Pazbi Zavatki

INNOVATION

'Standing still isn't an option. We are always looking AHEAD TO SEE THE NEXT BIG THING'

By Brian Tompkins, BCLA President and owner of TK&S Optometrists

There's an old saying that madness can be defined as repeatedly doing the same thing but expecting different results. I might have the odd 'mad professor' moment but when it comes to running a business I'd like to think I'm relatively sane.

I'm a big fan of technology. Whether it's the latest kitchen gadget or a must-have car accessory, I'm all over it.

It's the same with optometry and the way we interact with our patients.

In an age when competition is fierce and loyalty is low, the customer relationship is paramount. It's no longer enough to speak to someone every six months when they come in for an eye exam. We have to make them feel like one of the family.

Clearly, social media plays a huge part in this, allowing us to join in conversations with customers and communicate with them as people rather than patients.

We can show off our latest ranges and promote our monthly offers while discussing what they're having for dinner that night.

That's a huge shift, but for us it's just the tip of the iceberg. We want more. For us, standing still simply isn't an option: we are always looking ahead to see what's round the corner, searching for the next big thing.

The rise of the smartphone presented us with an opportunity to get in people's pockets, to be on the device they use the most. So we developed an app.

'Eye care from TK&S' gave information about the practice as well as hints and tips for patients, such as what to do if you get a contact lens stuck in your eye. It also showcased our latest products and encouraged people to visit the practice to view the full range.

Technology moves at a terrifying pace and keeping up is a challenge, but it's a challenge we embrace. We enjoy being pioneers, we revel in discovery and we have a thirst for being first.

Our Augmented Reality t-shirt was certainly pioneering. And it worked.

It showed the anatomy of the eye in a new and exciting way at events and exhibitions, using an image on a t-shirt as a barcode and playing 3D content through a smartphone. Fancy!

Keep pushing, keep innovating, keep challenging yourself. Most of all, enjoy it.

For more information visit
www.tks-optometrists.co.uk

ENGAGEMENT

THE KING THINKS HE'S IN CHARGE OF THE CASTLE!!

I am going to bring you back to what was mentioned about Engagement in the front of this book. It is not just an old witch tale, it is 100% a working fact. If you have ENGAGEMENT with your customers then growing your business is easier and faster for you.

Sometimes is can be hard to put yourself out there, take photos of yourself or be on a live video. Think about this though, you are the face of your business so why not use your face to advise instead of a logo. You can tell people more about your business, even how what you do can help your customer. These are things a logo can not do. Paying only bit of interest in someone else for even a small space of time, can benefit you ten fold.

We have only ever had, Newpaper Prints, Radio Ads and Television. Now we can answer back to the the adds.

MAKEING THE CUSTOMER THE CONTENT CREATOR

STRATEGY PULL OUTS

I got a slap for this part of the book, from a good friend. A real one in the face. This is where we give away, our secrets of time saving and stratigic planning. Follow this for the next twelve months and you will achive your goals

There are two pull out pages at the back of this book that have been created to help you to take control of yours social media. To help you manage your online presences. These pages are full of helpful sites that will show you what your internet rating is or how many people view your page and most importantly WHEN they view your page.

Strategy Is Key!

You can use this information and follow the begginners or advance strategies set out you help you manage what to do on different sites, when/ how much.

MONTH	TOOLS	BLOG	FACEBOOK
January	Meantion.net Aboutme.com	Blog about New Years Resolution	3 Posts a week
February	Likalizer Woorank	Blog about business events or News	1 video made and posted. 3 posts a week
March	RivalIQ PowToon	Follow other blogs similar to your business	Make and post deals only for Facebook Followers
April	AdwordTool GoogleAlerts	Blog about holiday deals	3 posts a week
May	Piktochart Talkwalker	Recommend a friend	Share Facebook page on other Social Media platforms
June	tchat.io klout	Blog about Holiday	Post about Holiday

Date:					
FB					
Posts					
Likes					
Comments					
Twitter					
Tweets					
Follows					
Lists					
SEO					
Blogs					
Directories					
Analytics					
Extras Instagram LI #FF					

These pages should help you use your collected data, be that your business information or customer information is a structured form, so you have a constant presence on social media.

Failt to Plan... Plan to Fail

STRATEGY ROUTES
SOCIAL MEDIA STRATEGY

Five Steps

- **Unifying Theme -** Internal / External

- **Platform Tactics -** With = WIN / Against = Love

- **Daily Tasks -** Momentum / Consistency / Systems

- **Listen -** Keywords, Reputation

- **Measurement -** Influence > Audience (Klout)
  Do they care? Where do they come from? Will they buy?

There are 1.65 billion active mobile social accounts globally.

Social networks earned £5.9 billion from advertising in 2015.

SOCIAL MEDIA FUNNEL

Facebook sits high in the funnel, and therefore drives greater awareness and more brand search terms, organic and paid.

Post Frequency
Facebook Adds
Liking Other Businesses
Benchmarking
Fan Acquisition
Understanding Algorithm

BUILD AUDIENCE

Newsfeed Reach
Social Reach
Search Ranking
Likes and Comments
Earned Media

ENGAGEMENT

Email Collection
Voucher Redemption
Purchase
Sharing
Retargeting

CONVERSION

TIME ON INVESTMENT

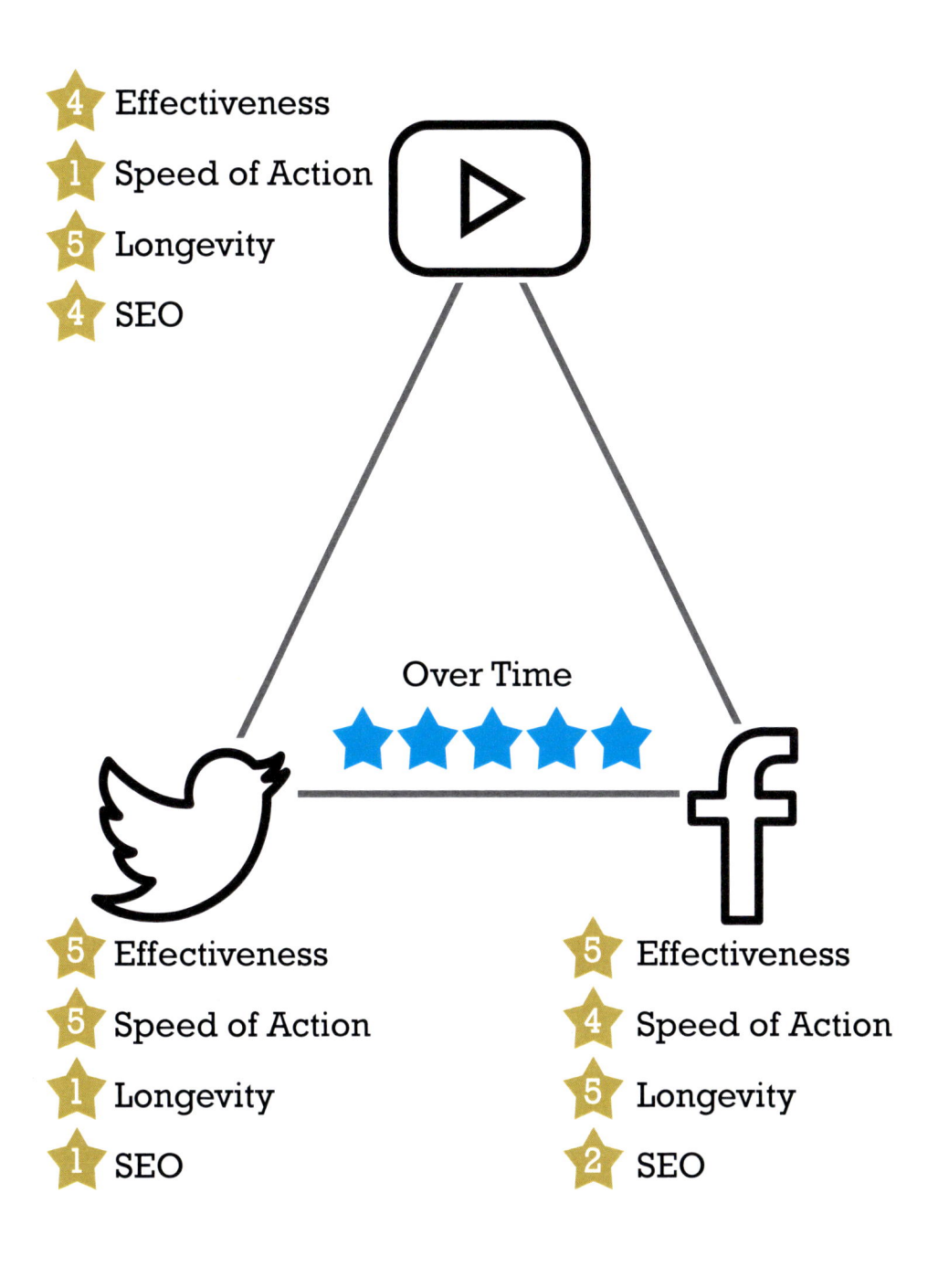

⭐ 4 Effectiveness
⭐ 1 Speed of Action
⭐ 5 Longevity
⭐ 4 SEO

Over Time
⭐⭐⭐⭐⭐

⭐ 5 Effectiveness
⭐ 5 Speed of Action
⭐ 1 Longevity
⭐ 1 SEO

⭐ 5 Effectiveness
⭐ 4 Speed of Action
⭐ 5 Longevity
⭐ 2 SEO

SOCIAL INSIGHT
DIGITAL TECHNOLOGY

Websites – almost everyone has one these days and if you don't, where have you been? I could reel off all the reasons you should have one, but I will make the assumption you already know the answer to that. Perhaps a better question to answer is why you need to invest in your website. By this I mean investing time, energy, effort and if your website is old and out-dated - money. This book outlines how important social media is and Garry will no doubt be encouraging you to devote a lot of your resources into this area. Of course, I agree wholeheartedly but, once built, websites can be forgotten and they shouldn't be.

Social media is constantly evolving and always on the move – people tweet, post and hashtag all day long and it is no doubt an important platform to manage because your brand's reputation is out there, being spoken about in a public space. How others view your company is crucial and social media is a space where you will need to try and manage how you are portrayed. However, a website is the one place where you are in complete control of what people see about you. Don't waste this opportunity! Your website should be personal to you – a reflection of your brand and a space where you can show, not just tell, that you have a fun/professional/knowledgeable/ high quality/good value (delete as appropriate) proposition. A good web designer will be able to craft the right image through use of colour, image and positioning in terms of user experience, as well as content.

If you have embraced the world of social media, you should let this benefit your website too. Link your social media feeds to your website - it is another opportunity to show that you know what your target audience like and want to see. After all, your website is the place people will come to when they are interested and ready to purchase, so linking social media content is another prospect to impress them and convert to sale.

Websites need all of the above and more. To be effective, you need to make sure you are refreshing your website too. Changing and updating elements of the site so that your target audience remain engaged and ensuring your website is still relevant with the changing times and trends. Plus, Google favours a relevant and constantly refreshed site. To do this it is advantageous for you to personally be in control. You don't want to have to pay every time you add something new to your website, otherwise you'd be spending a small fortune - that's why I train all my clients to use their Content Management System and update it themselves.

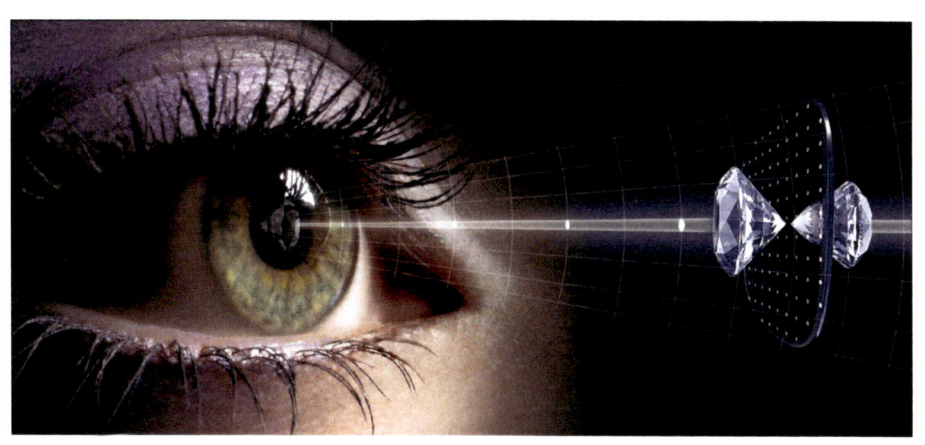

Finally, I advocate that data captures such as e-mail capture forms are not forgotten. In many ways they are one of the most important parts of your website, as they provide you with the opportunity to market to and learn more about your target audience. If you are writing great content on your blog and then sharing it on a mailing list this is an opportunity to generate repeat sales and more customers.

Many people think that once they have put up an initial cost for building a website they can forget about it, but websites are an opportunity to make or break your business. One that is responsive, relevant and engaging by being continually updated will take time and effort but will pay for itself. One that was built ten years ago and forgotten about will be at the bottom of Google's list and will cost you greatly.

Lucy Hall
Lucy's Web Designs

SEARCH ENGINE OPTIMISATION

Google is the biggest Search Engine in the world. It's so sophisticated that you will get the best results for your search queries. It has many add-ons such as Gmail, Google Drive, Google+ and many more.

YouTube is a Video Search Engine. It is owned by Google, so if you are maximising the potential on YouTube it will be reflected on Google.

Facebook is aiming to rival Google and be the best Search Engine available. Facebook is for pictures, text and videos. Having a Facebook

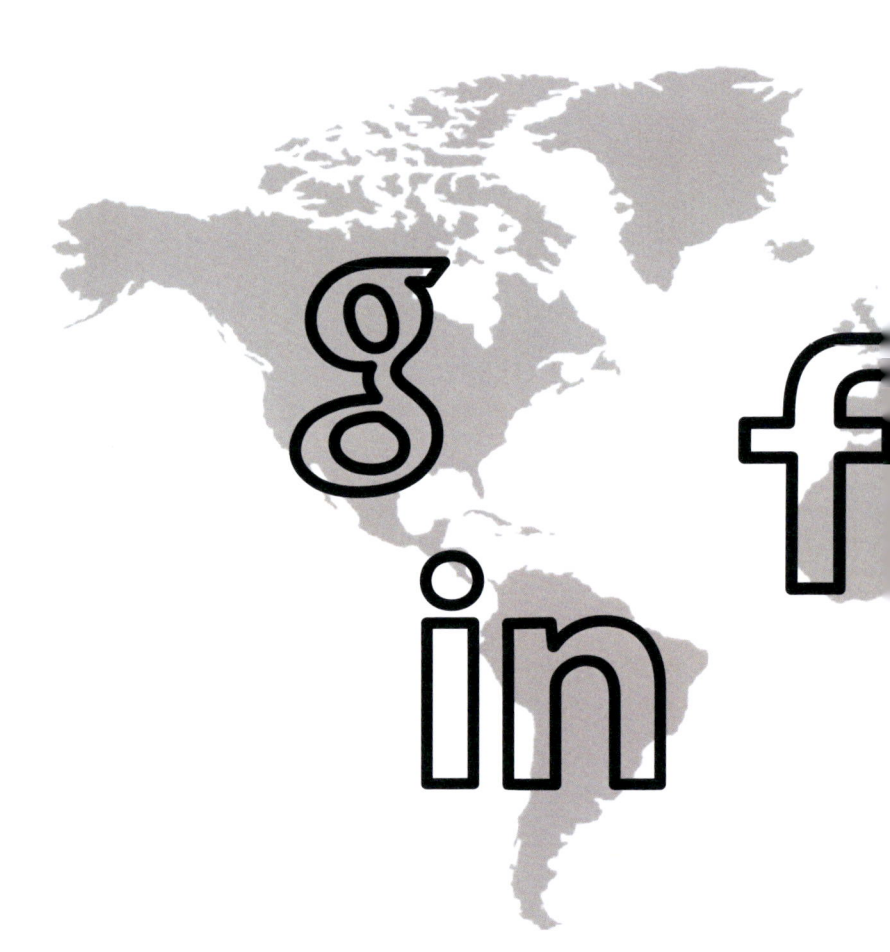

Fan page is great for the company's Search Engine Optimisation (SEO). Facebook also owns Instagram.

Twitter is a microblogging platform where you can share text, pictures and videos with one another. It doesn't have such a strong (SEO) hold as Facebook.

LinkedIn is the school uniform of Social Media. It is a platform where you can share news, stories and is the equivalent to having an online CV with skills and previous work experience. LinkedIn also owns Slideshare.

TREND JACKING

> **BEING THE OFFICIAL OPTICIAN OF THE BBC**

has been an eye-opening experience in itself. We've got journalists researching stories round the world, and walking past every journalist's monitor, I have now realised that everybody seems to have Twitter and they're all waiting for a story to break. At the time of writing this, there are 18.2 thousand tweets waiting to break and yesterday the passing of David Bowie created 6 million tweets. It was his brother who broke the news on Twitter and that's how the press got hold of the story.

In this friendly 24/7 online society, there isn't an internet resource that is superior to Twitter Trends for making current events and updated content stay pertinent. The ability of Twitter to track trends is such an unbelievably influential, but overlooked, tool. Users are able to set their accounts to track trends globally, nationwide and regionally. Learning to thrust with trends is a powerful tool.

You can manufacture content to different topics and demographics, as well as creating a buzz around your product or service between people who are not necessarily within your fan-base, and you can scale your sharing. The best thing is, you can jump on other people's content and retweet it, to give you respite from having to think about new ideas every day. It is harmless, as you're simply just using it to help out your brand. You will surely post new content from scratch; however in this case, you would use your content as a framework to tell a story.

One night I had a stroke of inspiration while watching Big Brother and tweeted about it. The next day I jumped on Twitter, and saw exactly what I expected to see; it was in the top 10 trending topics in the UK. It appeared to me that if customers wanted to talk about Big Brother, then marketers have to use the context of Big Brother in order to tell their stories. Could speaking about a current TV programme actually assist you in sunglasses? If you are imaginative enough then maybe it could. If you're a brand trying to jump on the bandwagon of Big Brother, the trick is to pick out the subtle connections rather than the obvious ones. Has your business ever felt like the Big Brother house? Have you got any plans to evict those old frames? Is there anyone in the house wearing glasses? We jumped on something very popular to make the story expand.

EXTROVERT & INTROVERT

Enthusiastic
Assertive
Talkative
Open
Less Private
More Accessible
Exposed

Preference for more stimulating environments

How successful communication improves patient understanding. We know by the very nature of our profession if somebody is extrovert or introvert. Why is this so important when it comes to social media? It's the introvert that will be absolutely offended if asked to be in a YouTube video whereas the extrovert loves the attention. For content the introvert

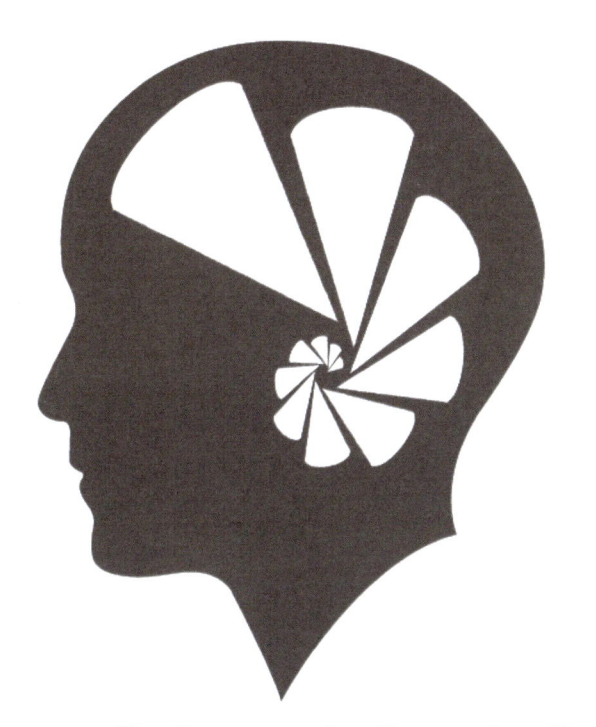

Analytical
Less Outspoken
Reserved
Sheltered
Enclosed
Less Accessible
More Private

Preference for less stimulating environments

is the person to ask. They will write you testimonials all day long or a review online. As for the extrovert they love videos and pictures. Give some thought to asking your patient to give you content. If you get it right the rewards can last for years and this is the stuff that converts to appointments and dispensing.

CYBERCRIME

THE IMPORTANCE OF BUSINESS SECURITY

By GoLive UK, UK Government Accredited Cyber Security Specialists

In today's business markets, it is essential all companies have a strong online presence. Businesses need to keep their web presence dynamic, updated with fresh content and to also maintain an active social media presence.

Social media forums such as Facebook, Twitter and LinkedIn are now actively being used to increase market share, attract prospective clients and keep existing ones engaged.

Today, the majority of businesses are moving away from traditional hard-disk storage devices to cloud-based solutions. Whilst there are many advantages to this, there is also the real constant threat of losing data and/or the data being stolen for malicious purposes that may damage a company's good reputation.

The internet is full of scams and hackers. Businesses are constantly under threat that they will lose their valuable data to cybercrime. This not only involves losing important data present on the website and on social media networks but also remote back-end data that might be extremely confidential.

Cybercrime in the UK now costs over £27 billion a year and in the U.S it is ranked by the FBI as one of the top law enforcement activities. We are all aware that many governments and multinational companies' websites have been a victim of cyber-attacks. There is a growing need for all businesses to urgently invest time and money to find the right solution to protect their online data.

Last year in the UK, Talk Talk faced one of the worst cyber-attacks of recent times - with an estimated four million customers being victims of this crime. There is a real fear that these customers' personal data, such as bank details, telephone numbers and email addresses, might have been accessed by cyber criminals for a variety of reasons.

Although it is impossible to prevent these attacks, companies can do a lot more to make sure their data is safe on the internet. Recent figures suggest that 97% of websites haven't updated their security ever since they went online. This period can be more than 5 years! In that time the hackers have constantly updated their skills making cybercrime easier.

Making sure a business is safe on the internet and well-protected does not actually cost a lot. It just requires a few precautionary steps and some thought to ensure data is safe. For example, updating security to the latest available version, making sure whilst sharing photos that a car number plate is not visible, ensuring passwords are stronger and not easy ones such as a date of birth, a partner's or a pet's name. This information is easily available on social media platforms and may make businesses/individuals vulnerable to an attack.

Also, it is important to be aware of unsolicited emails and emails that offer a cash incentive by clicking on a link. It is essential to ensure that the sender is genuine and is not using a scam email address.

If you have any concerns or queries regarding cybercrime and the security of your business online, then please contact Mr Ivan Yordanov. Email: ivan@goliveuk.com. www.goliveuk.com

SOCIAL MEDIA VS LEGAL RESPONSIBILITY

The use of social media can have many perils! The optometrist who went to a pub for lunch and a Facebook picture that landed him in hot water. This section should help avoid an unwelcome call from the GOC. Remember nothing is private online, optics is a regulated profession and has rules which need to be abided by. The old saying "a picture says 1,000 words" really comes into its own when we're talking about drugs, drink and sex.

- **Obtaining Valid Consent is imperative**
- **Do not give a patient's name online. Even leaving out a name, but speaking about an unusual patient could land you in hot water.**
- **Work within your limits of competency**
- **Do not give advice over and above your qualifications**
- **Always maintain adequate patient records**
- **If advice is offered on social media you still need it to be recorded on the patient's card**
- **If you do give advice using social media, make sure you come off public view. Practitioners should private message or speak on the phone.**
- **Maintain confidentiality and respect the privacy of your patients**

Do not damage the reputation of your profession through your conduct. No pictures of inappropriate behaviour! Tweets and videos can be even more tarnishing and people have lost jobs over them!

Questions: How to respond to complaints effectively, it's simple.
Answer: Take it off public view and communication privately.

USE YOUR COMMON SENSE!!!

SOCIAL MEDIA
SNAPCHAT

What is Snapchat?

Snapchat is a video messaging app where the users can send their friends short little videos or pictures that delete after they've been viewed. It's a highly popular app with the millennial market, but many media industry leaders are now seeing the potential in Snapchat, and are putting themselves onto the platform so they can be right where their target market is. While it's still a popular app, a lot of industries aren't seeing how they can market on Snapchat, thinking only the youth are on it to send messages to their friends. Optics could break this barrier and be known as an innovative industry, adapting to the changes and following their market.

How can Opticians use Snapchat?

You're probably thinking right now, how can opticians use Snapchat? That's a great question. Once you've got your customers following you, you need to be giving them value over Snapchat. The most obvious things are reminding patients they have an appointment. But not everyone will have their names on their profiles. I'd start by having Snapchat stories, showing the patients how to clean their contacts, how not to clean their glasses, what to do if you break your glasses, the possibilities are endless.

It's not just the How to… that you should be doing, showing you making a patient's glasses is a rare thing for opticians. Not many opticians can claim they've done that. You should be thinking outside the box, something that is behind the scenes. If you feel that it may not be interesting, there are people who'll want to see a different view into their opticians.

PERFECT SNAP OF SINITA IN VEGAS

BLOGS

A friend of mine once told me

"Sharing a blog is the best gift you can give your patients!"

I consider a blog to be the best investment that an optician can make to promote lenses, frames and every aspect of clinical work. My preferred platform to blog on is WordPress. Other platforms are available, but Google trusts WordPress more than others. With excellent content in a blog you can attract readers back to your site every month. This gets you all kinds of rewards. like higher ranking, more traffic, sales, email collection, amplification, and industry recognition.

Effective business blogging can be your digital voice, so by blogging about relevant and useful content you become the industry expert. How? Simply give the people what they want to read! When this happens, you can gain traffic as well as credibility, and then profits!

It is important to mention that according to Google Analytics, GoodLooking Optics are in the Top 60 keywords in Google searches including 'best optician in the world', 'carrera glasses logo' and 'optics london'. Out of those 60, 46 of those searches are from our blog which is attached to our website.

The best blogs have a killer heading. This is also the most important thing to help with your SEO. Make it something people will search for. For example "fun facts about glasses". However, don't be tempted to use too many tags, use one or two at the most and keep consistent with your keywords.

As for content, 300 to 800 words make up a good blog. Do not steal another person's blog off the internet and pass it off as your own. That is plagiarising and you can get caught, and possibly sued. Give your customers value. Don't just write a blog for the sake of it because you haven't blogged this week.

Where possible, insert two or three pictures and tag them well. This means embedding the picture in your blog with your keywords. Use bespoke images linked from Flickr and your desktop. As previously mentioned,

DO NOT STEAL PICTURES FROM GOOGLE!!

Your pictures should be used to perfectly illustrate the points that you are making in your blog.

There's an internet rule called 1%-9%-90%. This is basically a simple way of saying that 1% of people online will be content creators, writing blogs and cultivating their own audiences with self-promotion. A WordPress blog will be written by these "one percenters" who will have full control over the content within their blog. The 9% are those who want to write but do not want to take the leap into the creation of a full blog. These "nine percenters" aren't as focused on promotion and will often only provide content after some inspiration. They do not want to set time limits to their creations and instead are happy to share their blogs sporadically and receive feedback in a similar way. The "ninety percenters" are the meme-making majority. These people are those found on sites such as Tumblr or a microblogging site like Twitter. Here you can find blogs being retweeted many, many times. The "ninety percenters" are interested in collecting, commenting and republishing other people's work. They use these sites to express their interests in the hope of gaining recognition from like-minded people. Most of the content is not original and the more popular items will often be reblogged many times in its life-cycle.

To summarise, these are the three big reasons why you need to be blogging

- **Google loves fresh content. You get higher on the rankings as you are talking about a topic no one else is really talking about; OCT, blepharitis and transient bleariness**
- **Your content can be reused thousands of times on Twitter etc.**
- **To create engagement so people start to talk about your blog. You can respond to them in real time**

THE WORLD OF BLOGGING
BY SEV SAFER

I would like to cast your minds back to the simpler times…

Before social media over took the world and the most common worry became what to write on your status instead of what to have for dinner, When people put pen to paper and wrote their feelings down in secret diaries, others perhaps had written short stories as a hobby that just collected dust on their shelves and diaries that were hidden under beds contained more important information than google. Now bring yourself back to this moment… Where are your diaries? In the loft right? With all those problems that somehow became resolved over time, short stories that still never saw daylight and secrets that you thought were long gone only to be told as part of your wedding speech. Ever find yourself reading something online or in a magazine for example and thinking to yourself "I so can relate to that!" This is where I introduce you to the world of blogging.

Relating to something and knowing that there is another person who has had a similar thought process to you is one of the key success's to this field of social media. This is exactly how you draw your audience in and keep them captivated, find a theme and stick to it and you're half way to a successful blog!

As an international mum blogger you may ask yourself why it is that Garry asked me to write in this book that is aimed towards Opticians. It doesn't matter what end of the field you work in, the rules of blogging remain the same.

1. If you have answers or theories to subjects that you believe others would benefit from then write them down. Too often have I been criticised by people for sharing personal "mum experiences" with members of the public that I don't know. How many of those people did I help when I shared my experiences and stories? Thousands. How many people moaned that it's too personal to be shared with the world? Four.

2. Once you have written your blog, try and attach the correct image to go with the theme of the article. For example, if you're writing about which optical goggles are the best protection whilst on a skiing holiday, then the image should not be of a woman sunbathing wearing sunglasses.

3. Before you tell the world that a "New blog post has been uploaded!" Add it to your email newsletter and make sure that all areas of your social media have the link to the article directly. For example...

Twitter has a link in the edit profile section where you can input your recent blog post.

Happy Blogging to you all

Sev Safer
Digital Director @Lovingsocialmed
International Blogger
www.twobabiesonepram.com
@twobabiesonepram

Instagram has a similar layout to Twitter and you can insert your blog right here.

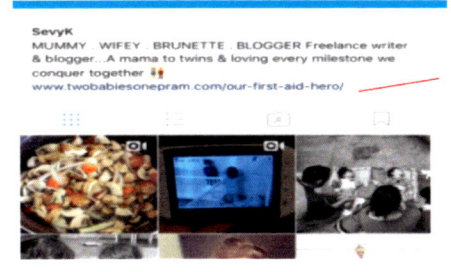

4. Now that you have attached the links to every social media you own, press that button and publish it. Let your friends share it with theirs and hope that they will pass it on, say thank you too all that shares it, comments and likes it.

5. Finally keep up to date with your blog, make sure that you're always one step ahead with writing and have your next one ready to launch when its convenient to your theme.

Share your ideas, stories or theories with the world. Don't keep them looked away in secret diaries waiting to be found by your great great grandchildren. Always remember this quote - By The Gingerbread Gem

To Blog =
To Share
To Connect
To Create
To Inspire

Sev Safer

OPTIMISE A BLOG
BY TARA HUSBAND

How to Optimise a Blog like an Aston Martin...
VMMMMMMMM

Most people will tell you how to optimise a blog like the "little engine that could". It implants into the web once or twice and hopefully Google or your friends will somehow see it. However, I prefer to set you up like an Aston Martin and make people stand back and say WOW! With these three stages, you will look like a pro, keep the engine running fast and beat out the competition.

> **Stage 1: The easiest way to optimise a blog is to create and understand your ongoing campaign.**

Your campaign is the outline of the information, sales strategy and conversations you will put out in order to achieve your company's online goal. For the month of January where people are making New Year's Resolutions, your campaign may be "LOOK at your weight dropping off." February it may be "Stare into the eyes of the one you love."

> **Stage 2: Branding is the next stage of development**

If you are doing the social media yourself, you can take a couple of photos of patients in their glasses that you want to display on social media. A theme is a great way to connect with your patients, such as a holiday theme with sunglasses, straw hats or beach clothes. Then send those to a graphic designer to develop content for every social media channel. You can create words to go along with your theme for posting. Perhaps add a coupon or two.

Ask the graphic designer to create and cut different photos out of the photos you give them plus using any new product you want to sell. Make sure you tell them you want photos to be in the correct size for Twitter, Instagram, Facebook and your blog. Having a month of these branded photos that correlate to your blog is what takes you to the "Yes, I will find you the right pair of glasses, Your Royal Highness" level.

Stage 3: Now it's time to start your engine

Now that the content is created, the blog is written and photos are in place, start your engine. Add your blog link to the original photos several times in your social media channels and ask questions so your users gather the information and pass it on. Add the blog to your email newsletter to keep it moving. Your blog content can also be broken down into mini posts on Instagram and Facebook. Keep the content, photos and blog link moving.

The biggest mistake people make is thinking that sharing once means people have seen it, however, optimisation has to be repeated. Thank everyone who shares, clicks and joins you in the ride!

In review, create a campaign every month so you are driving the optimisation of your blog and maximizing your social channels. Instead of being the "little engine that could" you will have the masterpiece of an Aston Martin.

Tara Husband
Digital Media with Edge
edgy.co
@TaraHusband

YELP

YELP IS A POWERFUL DIRECTORY

'Yelp is an American multinational corporation headquartered in San Francisco, California. It develops, hosts and markets Yelp.com and the Yelp mobile app, which publish crowd-sourced reviews about local businesses, as well as the online reservation service SeatMe and online food-delivery service Eat24.'

How is Yelp relevant to you? Yelp is one of the biggest directories out there, but there are a million others that do the same thing. The difference with Yelp is that they don't just want anyone reviewing businesses. You have to become a trusted reviewer.

At this stage you're probably thinking 'How do I become a trusted reviewer?' It's not as easy as just filling out your profile. You need to have friends on Yelp, and start reviewing wherever you go. It could be your dentist, favourite coffee shop, and after a few months, your reviews will start to show on their profiles.

One of my favourite parts of Yelp is that you can dispute any bad reviews. If someone has written something nasty about your practice, or a customer is unhappy, you can message them and see how you can change the negative review into a positive one. Of course, not everyone will reply and change their mind, but it's good for you to take the criticism given to you, so you and your staff will be able to learn from it.

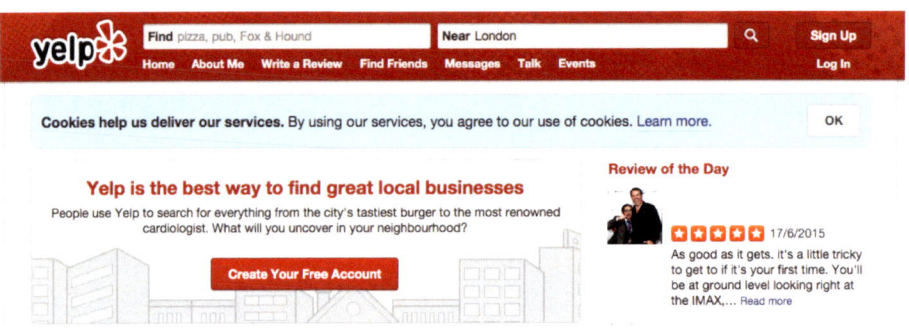

PINTREST

Pintrest tell you exsactly what it is from its name. It's a place you can pin your interests. Just a digital version of a real pin board. It is a site for sharing ideas. Some would say that Pintrest cannot be classed as a social media site, because of the way it works.

Unlike other sites, e.g Facebook and Twitter where you can direct your posts at who you want to see them and pay for it to be spread around multiple people's pages. Pintrest is not as structured. Due to this it is also not as limited by who can see the pins, or who could re-pin your pin.

IT IS THE INTERNETS VERSION OF 'WORD OF MOUTH'

If implemented on your websites or blog posts, Pinstrest could serve as a extra viewing platform for your products or ideas. People then who come on to your site and see a cool pair of glassess that they like, will pin it on to their profile. You can also pin the photo on to your own Pintrest proflie, but this won't make a different. The photo no matter who re-pins it will always link back to your site.

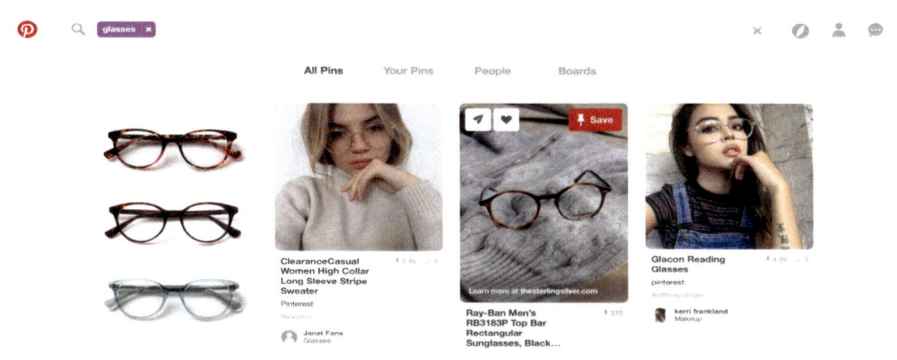

Past Pinning your products or ideas and tagging then like crazy, e.g #glasses. There is not much more you can do. It is out of your control. It is a social media site that is run by its customers and not the businesses.

Jordan M Jetley

FAQS

Do I need to have Social Media?

If you asked this question 10 years ago, you wouldn't have bothered with Social Media, but as of now, you can't afford not to have Social Media. Your customers are using it, your competitors are using it, so why aren't you using it? Many independents seem scared to use Social Media. They seem stuck in their ways and believe the marketing they did in 2004 is going to get them the same results in 2016, when in reality, putting themselves into the Yellow Pages is just wasting money, and preventing them from getting new business.

It's estimated that roughly 3-4 independents are closing down every week in the U.K, which is around 212 every year. The reason why? They can't compete with the big franchises. Specsavers have the finance and budget to pay for TV, radio and billboard adverts, which gives them the advantage. This is where Social Media comes into play; it gives you an even playing field to put your business out there.

I was in Dubai to do a talk, and before going I connected with 100 opticians in Dubai online, asking for an appointment. Only two opticians replied! Using the same experiment in London 78 out of 100 opticians replied. The telling thing: the chains replied within seconds and it was the independents who were slow to answer or did not get back at all.

You don't need to be the biggest, or the loudest optician online, you just need to build a relationship with your online customers, and show that there is a person behind the post. Your customers like you on Facebook, and engage with you on your page because they like your company, and want to be able to interact with you from wherever they want.

> **goodlooking optics**
> November 27, 2015
>
> So so happy with my new Gucci glasses, custom made and ready to take away within 20 minutes!!!! Thanks Gary and Lewis you did good
> 👍
> One very happy customer 😊

Using Goodlooking Optics as an example, we started to utilize social media while it was still very new, and it's benefitted us hugely. We get a number of customers coming in saying 'I found you from your videos on Facebook' and 'My friend checked in to your opticians, and I thought I'd give an independent a try' because we've built relationships with their friends, who keep coming back to Goodlooking Optics, and keep sharing their experience on Facebook.

As part of Facebook's policy, 'Facebook is a community where people use their authentic identities. We require people to provide the name they use in real life; that way, you always know who you're connecting with. This helps keep our community safe.'
- Facebook.

Do I need to be on all Social Media platforms?

No, you don't need to be on every platform, only the ones you think will benefit you. It's standard that you're on at least Facebook and Twitter. The majority of your customers will be on social media, and will be a user on at least one of these platforms.

Facebook's a definite must have platform for you to be using. It's by far the most popular platform, with 1.4 billion active users as of 2015. With that number of users, can you afford to not have a business page on there? It's free, so why wouldn't you? The only thing that will cost anything are adverts. Your average post is seen by less than 5% of your audience; it's now become a pay to play platform, where you have to spend if you want your posts seen.

Twitter, again is a must have to be using. It's not quite up there with Facebook, but still good enough that you should be using it. It's great for keeping an eye on your competitors, you can add them to a private list, and see what they're doing. If what you're doing isn't working, you can try and imitate what your rivals are doing. There's also the matter of engagement on Twitter. It's a much better platform for talking with your audience, or to start a conversation with your followers and other influencers in your community.

> **Just because a platform is there, doesn't mean you need to be using it.**

Pinterest, Instagram and LinkedIn are popular platforms, but do they work for opticians? If it's not where your target market is, then you don't need to be there!

PERSONAL PAGE

BUSINESS PAGE

78

Do I have to have a personal page to have a business page?

Yes, you need to have created a personal page to have a business page. A lot of people hear this, and are worried about embarrassing pictures showing onto their business page, but that's not the case. You can choose to post and have it appear as the page.

goodlooking optics
Published by ▇▇▇▇▇▇▇ [?] January 8 at 6:15pm

If you look at the top of the post, it says published by and the name of the user who posted it. I'm able to see who posted this status on Goodlooking Optics because I'm an admin on the page. For regular users on the page, no name only the date and time of the post is visible.

goodlooking optics
January 8 at 6:15pm

If you'd prefer to just have a separate account to be connected to your page, feel free to do that, but be careful. Facebook doesn't like it when users use false names, or their businesses' name for a personal account.

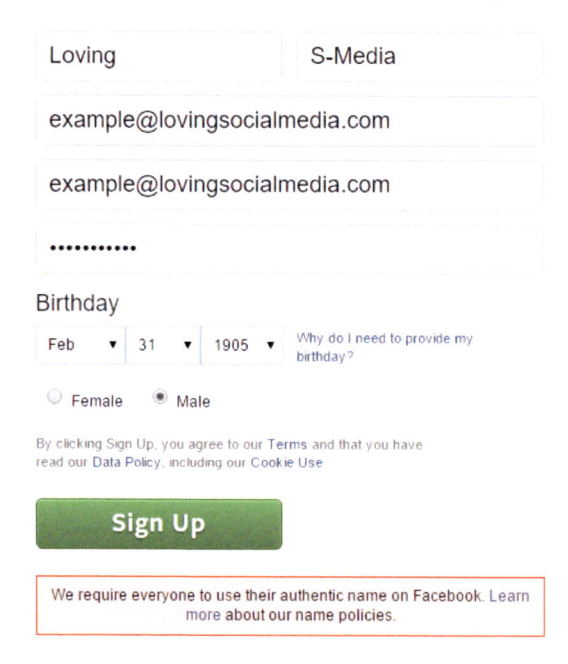

| Loving | S-Media |

example@lovingsocialmedia.com

example@lovingsocialmedia.com

••••••••••

Birthday

Feb ▼ 31 ▼ 1905 ▼   Why do I need to provide my birthday?

○ Female   ● Male

By clicking Sign Up, you agree to our Terms and that you have read our Data Policy, including our Cookie Use

Sign Up

We require everyone to use their authentic name on Facebook. Learn more about our name policies.

What is the hype about Social Media?

Social Media has changed the way we communicate. Instead of you recommending a product to your neighbour over the garden fence, social media means that now the recommendation to your neighbour turns into thousands of referrals to friends of friends of friends, etc. It gives real-time customer service. Answering your customers on social media can humanise your brand, keep existing customers and gain new ones!

Social Media ticks all the boxes of a classic marketing strategy:

Visibility = **Credibility** = Profitability

When one of your patients checks in or leaves a review on your Facebook page, it's a major benefit for your business. It moves your brand out of the circle of influence. For someone to come onto your page and see that people are leaving reviews and actually visiting the business, it gives you credibility and the more reviews you have, the better it looks on your page. When a customer checks in, everyone who is friends with them sees it on their timeline. If we take into consideration that the average adult is estimated to have 338 Facebook friends, having one person check into your page a week, 1,300+ users could see your business. When someone hears/sees a friend of theirs going into your business, it's the equivalent of a recommendation to your neighbour over the garden fence!

THE THREE PERCEPTUAL CHANNELS

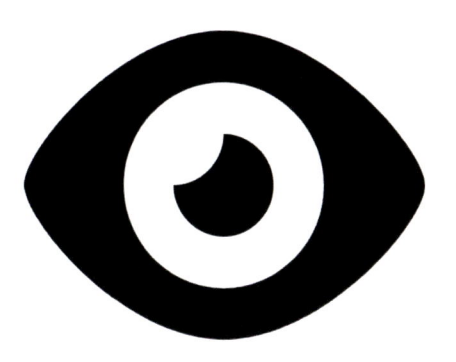

Visual
Printed materials, facial expressions, body language - what is seen - Pinterest

Kinesthetic
Emotions, actions, movement, task, smell - what is felt - YouTube

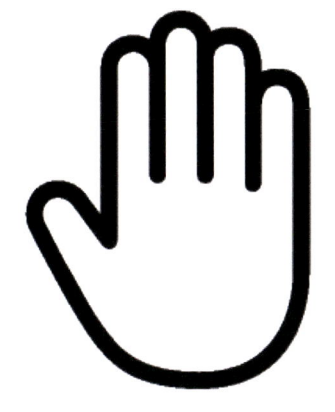

Auditory
Spoken words, sounds - what is heard and said - Facebook

CHEAT SHEETS

Twitter

Why do it?
It raises your visibility locally to the right people.
Unfollow/Follow App – The Unfollow app allows you to unfollow users who you are following, but haven't followed back. You can also follow users who are following you on the app. The unfollow app is useful because it is simple to use and less time-consuming than scrolling through your following list and unfollowing every account that hasn't followed you back.

Likealyzer

Why do it?
Unless your Facebook fan page is effective, there's no point.
Get your score to 60+.
Likealyzer helps assess your Facebook page to see what you're doing right with your page and what you can improve on. Likealyzer will score your page on a scale from 1-100. If your Likealyzer score is in the 70+ range, then you're running your page well, but you can still improve. If your score is below 50, then you will have to drastically improve your page and take their advice to ensure your page gets into the higher ranks of Likealyzer.

Klout (browser/App)

Why do it?
It measures your effectiveness.
Klout checks your social media score to see how big an influence you are on social media. Klout measures your score on a scale from 1-100, with 100 being the best, and 1 being the worst. If you have a low following on your social media platforms, you're going to have a low Klout following. Those with a following that constantly mentions or replies to them will have a higher Klout score due to the influence they hold over their followers.

Yelp

Why do it?
It helps increase your Google ranking. Yelp is a directory where you can register your business, review other businesses or look for a business e.g. Café in Stoke-on-Trent. If your business is at the top of the search results on Yelp, then you're running your business well, while if your'e not very high, you're not doing very well and need to get your customers to add a review to your Yelp page.

Hub Spot / Moz Local

Why do it?
It shows you where you're placed in your local area.
These sites are free tools which analyses your account an website.

Hub Spot: GENERATE LEADS, CLOSE DEALS & MANAGE YOUR PIPELINE WITH THE HUBSPOT GROWTH STACK.

Moz Local: MOZ LOCAL HELPS LOCAL SEATCH ENGINES – AND NEW CUSTOMERS – FIND YOUR BUSINESS ONLINE.

Reviews.co.uk

Why do it?
It gets you higher on Google ranking.
Reviews is a webpage that gathers reviews from shoppers to help increase businesses and put them further out in the market. Reviews doesn't want any bots on their pages so they ask for proof of purchase so you can write a review. This website is a great page to look for feedback from real customers, or can be used to show your terrific reviews on your website. Anybody can ask friends to go give them amazing reviews on any other directory, but the fact that Reviews actually checks that they've used the company rubs off greatly on the business.

CHEAT SHEETS
MEASURING YOUR SUCCESS

You've been reading through this book, and might have thought once or twice 'It's all well and good you telling us this information, but how will we know if it's actually working? How will we know if it's helping our business or not?'

There are different ways you can see if what you're putting into place is actually working. For Facebook users, your best tool is Insights. Insights lets you track the number of active users on your page, and how well your posts are doing. It's fairly easy to access. Take a look at the top menu and you should spot Insights straight away.

This is what it looks like when you go into your page's Insights any time. You're able to see how much you've grown, the number of people you've reached anytime in the last year and the number of engagements on your page.

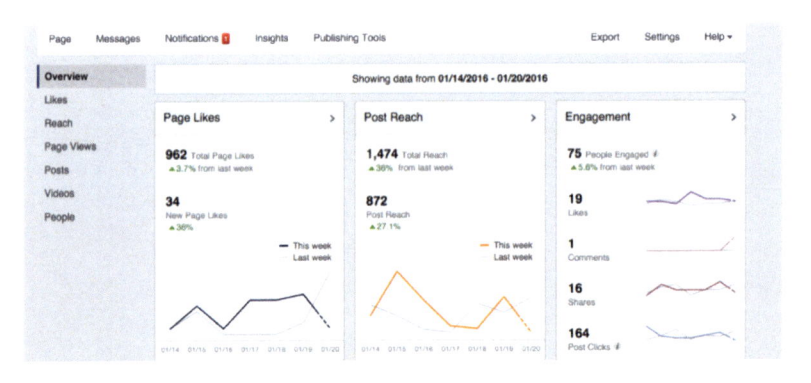

From these results, you can see there was a significant growth in all categories, then towards the end of the month, it dropped off. Looking at this, they can go back to the posts and see what they did wrong that caused them to drop off.

Published	Post	Type	Targeting	Reach	Engagement	Promote
01/20/2016 1:41 pm	25% off your Fabris Lane order a t 100% Optical*			30	0 / 0	Boost Post
01/20/2016 11:58 am	The BB1510, available at a Boot h&Bruce stockist near you! And s			13	1 / 1	Boost Post

Further down the page, you can actually follow the graph and see where we dropped off. Our highest point was from the boosted posts, so it was expected the posts would drop off back to the usual 2% of our audience seeing it organically.

Twitter Analytics is fairly easy to get into. As soon as you load the page, this should be the first thing you see, or something similar. These are the key statistics for your Twitter account over the last 28 days, put right in front of you without you having to look for it. Using these as an example, January was not as popular as December, even though we're halfway through.

Going through the homepage, it gives you the highlights and summary each month, and makes it easier for you to compare how well you've done over the past months. The summary includes number of tweets, mentions, impressions, profile visits and new followers.

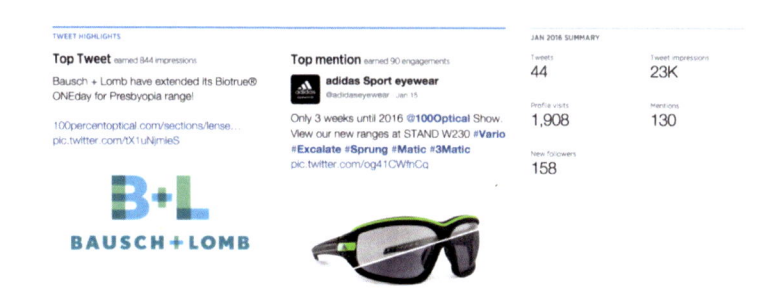

Google Analytics is by far the most important. This lets you know if all the hard work and effort on social media isn't wasted, and that you're raising your visibility. On the homepage, it gives you the key points such as users on your website, how long they were spending, how many page visits per session.

Sessions	Users	Page Views
1,634	1,450	2,933
Pages/Session	Avg. Session Duration	Bounce Rate
1.79	00:01:09	75.03%

% New Sessions
84.58%

This is one of the best parts of Google analytics, and something everyone should be looking at when checking their analytics. You're able to see how many keywords and phrases that you're ranked for, and where in the search engines they are. This account has over 61 unique keywords, with nearly all at the top of the first page.

Another great feature about analytics is to track where your referrals to your website are coming through, and specifically what social networks are sending traffic through. Out of 1,361 users, 125 were from social media, with the majority coming through Twitter.

All these numbers count for nothing, unless you see a turn-over in your profits!

HELPFUL LINKS

#askgaryvee
www.youtube.com/user/GaryVaynerchuk

#askgaryvee is a show on YouTube run by the heavyweight of the social media world, Gary Vaynerchuk. The show is a perfect way to keep your knowledge up-to-date on everything social media and more. You can also find more great content on Gary Vaynerchuk's YouTube channel. Go take a look!

Social Media Examiner
www.socialmediaexaminer.com

Social Media Examiner has a hub of insightful information about everything social media, ranging from how to optimise your social media experience and content, to using social media to have fun. Access their free podcasts and learn even more about social media.

Mari Smith
www.marismith.com

Mari Smith, aka "The Queen of Facebook", is one of the world's leading experts in Facebook marketing. Want to learn more? Mari Smith can teach you everything she knows, be that through her book, blog or live

---

There is nearly 2.5 Billion active users on social media, a global penetration of 30%

DIGITAL GLOSSARY

■ B2B
Business to business.

■ B2C
Business to consumer.

■ Content
The text, pictures, videos and sounds you use.

■ Cloud-based Solution
Information that you can retrieve on the internet.

■ Digital
Not on paper.

■ Digital Credibility
Your Klout score.

■ Engagement
Having a conversation online.

■ Fan/Follower Acquisition
More visibility with followers, likes and views measurable by numbers.

■ Fiverr.com
A website to get digital things done on the cheap. Graphic Design, Web design etc.

■ Google Analytics
Google's free data collection service. Google Analytics tells us how individuals have arrived at our website, how long they stayed and a feast of other really great information for measuring your effectiveness.

■ @
The beginning of your Twitter address. Example @opticians .

■ Organic
Natural search without you having to pay.

■ Platform
Another word for what you are using on the web i.e Facebook, Twitter and websites.

■ Pixal
This a a new software inplimented on Facebook to follow your cookies!

■ PPC
Pay per click.

■ Re-targeting
New visitors knowingly get any information about what you care about and following you around.

■ SEO
Search engine optimisation.

■ Strategy
Plan of execution in advance.

■ Social Media
Any digital platform that you can have communication - backwards and forwards.

■ Traffic
Individuals coming to your platform and website. Be careful they could be non-human too!

■ Unifying theme
Having all your platforms looking the same.

■ Vimeo
Alternative to YouTube.

■
A word or phrase preceded by a hash sign (#), used on social media websites and applications, to identify messages on a specific topic.

> If you find any words in the book you are unfamiliar with, send me a tweet @opticians and ask

TWEET US
ANY
SOCIAL MEDIA QUESTION RELATED TO OPTICS AND WE'LL GET BACK TO YOU @LOVINGSOCIALMED

Loving Social Media

020 3846 8888

HALL OF FAME

Score	Name	Followers
68	Opticians	18.7k
68	RNIB	29.2K
65	ray_ban	488.4k
63	2020mag	14.3k
61	btoptom	2,626
60	AntoniaChitty	9,075
56	1eyeinrumney	890
56	fightforsightUK	6,128
51	OPTOMETRISTS	8,625
50	MOSCOT	5,063
50	MacularSociety	5,063
49	Luxottica	34.4k
48	TheEyebrights	2500
47	The_AOP	3215
47	100Optical	4611
47	CollegeOptomUK	5266
45	kirkandkirk	1603
45	OptometRRy	4025
45	JDoyle_Optician	1888
45	eyecarefaq	1740
43	MembershipAbdo	1605
42	SpecsNetwork	1883
43	TKSOptometrists	1869
39	NathanGarnett	1153
37	theeyegeek	1461
36	essiloruk	1031

I have left the rough diamond jewel in the crown to the last page! These are the movers, shakers and influencers. If you truly want to get a message across you need to engage with these influencers!

You can bore people to death with adverts or you can story tell....

To be continued...

"Give so much value that the patient does not need to ask your advice any more!"

Garry K